Peter Owen Jones is an author, television presenter and Anglican clergyman. He has presented various acclaimed BBC TV series, including 'Extreme Pilgrim', 'Around the World in 80 Faiths, and 'How to Live a Simple Life'. An avid walker, he has contributed suggested walks to the *Sunday Times* and is the author of many books, including *Letters from an Extreme Pilgrim*. He lives on the edge of the Sussex Downs.

Pathlands

Pathlands

21 tranquil walks among
the villages of Britain

PETER OWEN JONES

LONDON · SYDNEY · AUCKLAND · JOHANNESBURG

1 3 5 7 9 10 8 6 4 2

Rider, an imprint of Ebury Publishing,
20 Vauxhall Bridge Road,
London SW1V 2SA

Rider is part of the Penguin Random House group of companies
whose addresses can be found at global.penguinrandomhouse.com

First published by Rider in 2015. This edition published in 2017

www.eburypublishing.co.uk

A CIP catalogue record for this book is available from the
British Library

ISBN 9781846044441

Printed and bound by Clays Ltd, St Ives PLC

Penguin Random House is committed to a
sustainable future for our business, our readers
and our planet. This book is made from Forest
Stewardship Council® certified paper.

In order to enjoy the walks described in this book, none of them
should be attempted without the relevant Ordinance Survey map
(or, in this case of Walk 7, the States of Guernsey official map),
keeping to marked rights of way.

*For my sister, Sarah Jane
and my brothers, David and Tim*

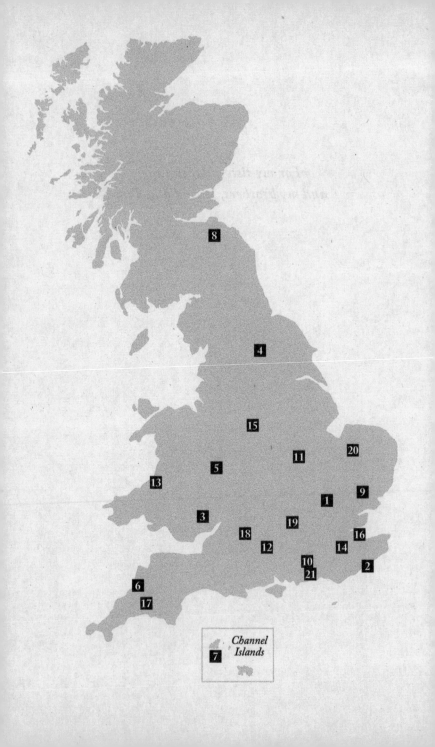

Contents

Preface

They say there is no wind on the moon. Can you imagine the silence without it? It must be as thick as honey and the monotony would, in time, leave you aching for thunder – it is silence that drives most men mad. Can there be memory without movement? Maybe it is only artists who can manage it, stealing light from time and, somehow, turning the sea solid without any of us really noticing that this is what they have done.

Hanging in an upstairs dining room in the Smithy Arms in Welcombe, Devon are two prints, both taken from original paintings of the moon which were, themselves, painted from photographs brought back from the Apollo missions of the sixties and seventies. I love them being there, in that room, on that wall, on Planet Earth. Here is a reminder that there are many other worlds, many other realities, so much land and sky we haven't even imagined yet.

Maybe, several centuries from now, human beings will look back and find it rather endearing that we should still walk to explore; that at the beginning of the third millennium men and women still strived to walk across the poles, still set off for the last few remaining deep unmapped valleys of the

Himalayas on foot. If there is an eternal truth, maybe it is this: that we can learn from those who have been there. We can understand how broad it is, how high it is, how steep it is from looking at a map. We can go online and look at endless pictures of a thousand places we have never been to, but we can have no memories of a place until we have walked within it.

In his seminal book *Guns, Germs and Steel* Jared Diamond explains how we walked out of Africa, then into Asia, then Australasia and Europe. Finally, we walked over the ice from what is now Russia into Alaska, from there down through North America, eventually reaching Cape Horn. I remember as a child walking out into the fields at the back of the house. Clambering over gates and through the gaps in hedges, past ponds, along those tracks that only the farmers use to take them from field to field until I reached an abandoned barn that sat sheltered next to a lonely pond enclosed in trees on the top of a rise. Looking south I could see the blurred folds of land running down from the Weald. It called me, called me into the distance, into the unknown. It is that call in all of us that has taken us to walk the furthest shores of this planet, into the mystery of the vastness of space and purpose of atoms.

We see Australia as a land of enormous sheep stations and massive fields of wheat, but 230 years ago, the men and women living there were hunter-gatherers, who walked the land and passed down their paths in songs and dreams. The last of these wanderers, the Pintubi, were 'brought in' by Land Rover in 1965 by patrol officers of Australia's Northern Territory. Getting into that Land Rover would have been the first time those men, women and children had moved without walking.

Until the invention of Land Rovers, trains and bicycles the rich rode on horseback, and those who did not have the means to own a horse walked.

As a child I remember going to an exhibition about the history of the village I grew up in. There, above a pair of tattered shoes I found the life story of a cobbler who had lived in the village. Once a week he would walk twenty-eight miles up to London to sell his shoes, and would walk back the next day. He made this journey every week of his adult life until he died in his eighties.

Up until the First World War, if you ventured out on to one of the main routes anywhere in the world you would have found them full of people walking. Many people on the planet still walk. Four years ago, I was staying in a cave just outside a village in the foothills of the Himalayas in India. Each morning, all the unmarried young women would file past heading into the hills to collect wood, returning at about four o'clock each day with these huge bundles strapped on their backs. At three o'clock in the afternoon during term time in India, the edges of the roads fill up with files of children in bright red and yellow blazers returning home from school. Some walk a twelve-mile round trip every day.

Walking is not just about going from here to there: it is about what we encounter on the way, both externally and internally. When we reach the top of the hill alone and stand and watch the sunrise, what we are taking part in is another beginning – the birth of a brand new day. It invites us to let go of some of the past, to understand that, in one life, there are so many beginnings. We are born fluent in feeling. Before we can speak, we can feel – we feel joy, delight, tenderness, pain, guilt, wonder. The tree does not think her way into the light; she feels it. The river does not think his way to the sea. Our feelings are the wellsprings of our being. Whilst we might say we are looking at the view, what we are really doing is feeling it, taking part in it; the truth is, we are at that moment in relationship with it.

I could not have written this book had I not been born into a land that contains an intimate lattice of paths. The paths of the British mainland are one of the greatest jewels and legacies left to us by all who have walked them, all who have honoured and upheld their existence over the centuries, and there is no other country on the planet that has such an intimate network of public footpaths. There are still some pathways in the major cities of mainland Britain, a hangover perhaps from the time when outlying villages were absorbed into expanding urban areas. The fact that it is possible to walk legally and unhindered from one end of the country to the other on a network of interlinking paths is something I had not considered to be a vital constituent of freedom until I had visited lands where no such network of paths exists. In their absence, communities are confined, even in the countryside, to roads, pavements and shopping malls. Freedom of movement is utterly essential to our experience of being free; it is one of the most important, yet least enshrined, human rights. This freedom has, in certain places, been hard won by acts of 'mass trespass', most notably on to Kinder Scout in the Peak District on 24 April 1932. There is almost an awkward pathos that hangs in the air in those where freedom to roam is denied. Nowhere for me is this more apparent than in Northern Ireland, where the highly toxic religious segregation has meant that it is not possible to walk across the fields from one village to another. Communities live in cages. Human beings, along with all other life forms, do not do well in cages. Pathways are not just incidental dotted lines on a map; they are an intimate reality of freedom. Opening a few paths between communities in Northern Ireland would go a long way towards the making of peace on the ground, not just in the mind.

Between seven and eight million people in the UK go for a walk on any given weekend, many travelling out from cities to walk in the hills and fields. The liberation many people sense from walking all day alone is the freedom from being observed, from being judged. You can sing as loudly as you care to, shout at the wind, lie down and sleep, make love, eat with your mouth open, piss where you want to and you will not be arrested for doing so. It was the Romantic poets who are the fathers and mothers of today's walkers. It was Wordsworth, Shelley and Keats who elected to leave the confines of their urban environments and, quite literally, take to the hills to see their humanity reflected in the natural world. Before then, walking was predominantly considered an arduous necessity, though of course there were exceptions. The very un-Romantic Dr Samuel Johnson is known to have rolled down a hillside on one of his country rambles. The Romantic poets changed the nature of walking into an essential experience, seeing it as time out from papers, shovels and smoke, just as for us it is an escape from screens, machines and malls. It was, in part, their reaction to the industrialisation, to pollution of the emerging utilitarian, commercial and industrial society. The Industrial Revolution fostered the world we live in today, beginning a process that has increasingly distanced human beings from the natural rhythm of the seasons and the apparent inconsistencies of the weather. Factories and offices are environments we believe we can control; they offer a great deal more certainty than the fields. It is easy, perhaps all too easy, to romanticise the natural world and it is one of our most enduring characteristics to see this planet as beautiful. Yet we inhabit a brutal and unpredictable Earth, which has fathered and mothered each one of us. You would have to have a heart of steel not to be enchanted by bluebell woods in May, but you need a heart of steel to traverse the Cuillin Ridge in the midst of a November storm. It is worth remembering that walkers still die each year: some from exposure, some from falls, and some from being attacked by animals as they 'wander lonely as a cloud' through their territory.

When we walk, we walk through two landscapes: an exterior land of trees, seas, cities, mountains and fields and along the paths that lead into our own interior world. Whilst we do walk through history, both natural history and the history imprinted on the land by all who have been here before us, most of us do not walk consciously through the past unless, of course, that is what we are looking for. Most of us do not walk knowingly through geology or sociology; we walk to know the present better than we did before – to be brought into its presence. Once we can find the present, we become present. This also means knowing our agendas, hurts, angers and desires. In that sense, walking can be tremendously healing because it illuminates what we are carrying – the weight of anger, resentment and bitterness, the heavy chains of history. As St Francis of Assisi said 'Solvitur ambulando' – it can be solved by walking. I have left the house many times embittered, and returned smiling and better able to be generous to those who have caused me pain, whilst appreciating more keenly that I am no different in my capacity to do the same. I also leave the house never quite knowing what I am about to encounter, what I will see, hear, smell; there is nothing perhaps as calming as a still summer's day – but it can be that only if I can accept its gift. And if there is nothing so melancholic as a sheep standing alone in the rain, there is something so renewing about clouds that pass and leave in their wake a shining new world. Once I am able to see it, to enter the state of wonder, the division between myself and the distant folding land, the cliffs and the dead leaves is dissolved; this state of communion is one of the most profound gifts that walking can give. The reason why so many of us walk is that we return home stilled and renewed but, most of all, we have allowed ourselves, however fleetingly, to wonder – and that, perhaps, is the food the gods are feasting on.

I started walking seriously every day having had Bell's palsy. My face was paralysed and it was like entering an exhausted twilight. I had been broken by the work I was doing and my marriage was also, very sadly, caving in under the strain. As a child I used to walk almost every day out into the fields that lay beyond the back of the house I grew up in but, with all the cares of raising a family and struggling financially to keep afloat, I had let this go. The doctors put me on a strict regime of steroids and antivirals. After about two weeks, I woke up one morning and knew I had to go for a walk – and it was walking that brought me back to life; it gave me the space to reflect and begin to unknot all that had become tangled and to find sweetness again. I now live on the South Downs in southern England and walk just about every day. What I have learned is that each time I set off I walk into a new world. Yes, there is the intimate knowledge that comes with time but each day is profoundly different from the one that went before. The land changes during the night: butter-flies arrive, fruit ripens, the wind rips leaves, the rain polishes fields. My lovely children occasionally berate me for taking the same walk every day, but it isn't the same walk. It is the same path, but it is always a different walk.

In this book there are twenty-one walks, each of them taking a different path into the exterior and the interior. I have chosen not to walk the well-trodden paths of the National Parks but the everyday paths between villages that people use to walk their dogs or simply go for a Sunday stroll: these are the paths that form, as I have said, the bedrock of the sense of freedom in this land. Every walk is a circular walk and sometimes I have taken to minor roads, especially on the island of Guernsey, where there are very few sections of public footpaths.

I would like to thank all who work so hard to keep the paths open: The Ramblers (previously the Ramblers' Association) and all of those who live in the villages and towns and have an affection for the paths that they use, sometimes on a daily basis. Also the map-makers whose attention to detail means that we can all find our way around a place that we have no knowledge of. I must thank the cattle that provided the leather for the bootmakers who kept my feet dry; the sheep, and the weavers who make the tightly woven woollen tops that kept me warm; the musicians who produced wonderful albums that filled many of the long journeys especially Max Mezzowave, Carrie Tree, John Mayall, Norah Jones and Bill Evans. And finally I thank my mother Daphne, who had the good sense and courage to allow me to roam as a boy on my own in the fields and valleys that backed on to our house: it is from there that all these journeys begin.

Barwick Ford, Hertfordshire

Two inches out

Fords are surely points where the wild crosses the man-made. It is no more than a brief encounter, the water hurrying past as if it is naked, heading between the tarmac back into the safe keeping of overgrown banks and overhanging branches. Roads and paths create the illusion that the land is known, yet really very little of it is seen: there are so many corners that none of us go into for years on end. The copse between fields, the steep wooded slopes, abandoned railway embankments, bogs and thickets of gorse.

As a younger man I would leave the path and venture into the depths of woodlands, and in one wood on the Surrey–Sussex border I found a garden. The first hint was a rotting shed hidden, almost locked into some overgrown pines; the slats had come loose and most of the timbers were crumbling. I slipped in through a gap in the wooden walls. Inside was one garden roller covered in ivy and a couple of broken flowerpots.

Just beyond the shed I could see the silver surface of a long pond caught between some low-hanging branches; it was full of weed and snakes. The pond had been imagined: because at the far end the water slid down through a sluice in a man-made bank and disappeared into a thicket of bamboo. The garden came alive in the spring. A huge cherry tree bloomed over the pond and the land above it had been planted with rhododendrons, all of them flowering in every different size and colour, pinks, deep reds, purples and soft yellows, some of them with blooms the size of footballs, and I have seen nothing like them since. There had been paths through the garden but they were overgrown with brambles and blackthorn, the only clear space was one bank of moss which sat under an oak just above the pond. The garden was an exotic oasis hidden in the heart of an English wood.

Although being a place on the map, Barwick Ford is no more than a farm and a ford on the River Rib. The path crosses the road about one hundred yards above the ford and rises steeply at first through a wood, and then runs through a gloomy thicket where the white confetti petals of blackthorn were scattered all over the dark earth. At the end of this twisting tunnel there is scruffy field which leads down to a basking river reflecting Constable clouds, but there was an almost continual thunder. Every three minutes or so a plane would fly directly overhead; they must have been taking off from Luton or Stansted crammed with suitcases full of shorts, bikinis, towels and sun cream as the pale passengers headed south for some easy warmth. The gardener who was digging a vegetable patch on the other side of a fence at the end of the field was wearing no more than jeans and a T-shirt, his forearms were the size of bowling balls wrapped in jagged tattoos. I asked what he was planting. He said he was just clearing the ground and that last year the soft fruit had been very good, which seemed a little strange as the fruit cage behind him had nothing in it. On the lawn behind him stood a life size sculpture of a red deer made entirely of horseshoes and, next to the deer reclining in the middle of a flowerbed was a large pixie – and rising up in the middle of another flower bed in front of the pixie was an entire stone frame of a monastic doorway without a door. I would love to have seen the garden in the moonlight.

Not far from the garden, the path winds through a small copse then opens out on to farmland. In the winter it would be bleak here but now the wheat and barley leaves are filling out, the stems are thickening, the cereal fields are rising and changing colour; in the early dusk they can become almost blue. Most of the colours here live in the ditches, in, buttercups, bluebells, campion, cow parsley and the white flowers of Jack-by-the-hedge and the heady almond souk hanging around the hawthorn trees that were just tipping into flower. The sunshine had brought out the butterflies, orange-tips, small and green-veined whites and a rabble of small tortoiseshells hunting for food and dancing for sex. Female butterflies lay about one hundred eggs, but only two result in butterflies that will make it into the air. As the path approached the brow of the hill a light breeze rippled the fields: it was cold air coming in from the north. And the blue in the sky tightened and deepened. I love the way we cannot see through it: that the stars still shine in the daytime but we just can't see them through the blue and how the moon sleeps in a clear sky. Lying under a few ragged trees on the brow of the hill is a little pond. This mother that has borne life untold now lies barren; her womb has become a grave. Once she bore frogs, suckled nymphs, skaters and newts, her bed gave rest to wandering mallards and her summer table seethed with midges and dancing bats. Now she barely breathes and is covered in rancid sores. Rotting on the surface of the water was the tell-tale green and yellow flesh of algal blooms that had gorged themselves on nitrate fertiliser which, having been spread over the fields, seeps into the water through the soil. The evidence was there on the path, which was peppered with small white pellets, a poisonous sugar, and further on a few ice-like lumps that had fallen into the ruts and grass.

New oak leaves are almost translucent, they have a green that you look into rather than at and when they are held against a bluebell sky each colour feasts off the other: it is a meeting of skin. I don't know exactly how long I stood under a line of oaks looking up into this picture before I took the path that turns towards Bartram's Wood. The cream-coloured shed on the edge of the wood gave absolutely no indication of its purpose; it was boarded up and didn't appear to have a door. Behind it lay a sweeping entrance into the wood, which was largely silent.

Just beyond the entrance, growing in between strands of brushwood stood about ten early purple orchids as tall as bluebells. Orchid flowers can vary in colour and some are almost white, but these ones were pure purple and their scent lay somewhere between hay and honey. Beyond the wood the path ran between several great yellow lakes of oilseed rape; it was the height of my shoulders, growing right up to the path and for several hundred yards I was locked into a primary world consisting of just yellow and blue. When the oilseed rape is in flower it smells sweet, but when the seedpods arrive it rots the air around it, turning it sour and acrid.

The yellowhammer just seemed lonely; there are very few birds here. It flew across the path and then doubled back and landed twenty feet in front of me. Once when I was trying to untangle a lamb from some wire I found a yellowhammer's nest. They nest on the ground; this was a bowl of stems and leaves stitched into the grass, and hidden away between a ditch and hedge.

On the other side of a deep ditch running down towards Much Hadhdam the sun flashed against the blank windows of a new barn conversion. The black wooden walls were completely surrounded by newly laid turf that looked as if it had been washed and sterilised. It must be surreal, moving into an old building that no one has ever lived in. From here the path seemingly evaporated so I followed the hedge around the side of field and watched as a tawny owl broke cover and bounced through the air flying silently back towards the barn conversion. Luckily there was a gap in the hedge with a road on the other side of it and not far from where I had crawled through was the path down to Moat Farm.

Only an idiot would ask a woman standing on a bridge over a moat if this was Moat Farm, but she took the question in good humour and we talked for a while. She told me that in the harsh winter of a couple of years back all the carp had died as the moat had remained frozen over for a month or more. She also went on to say that every year on 13 February the ghost of a woman rises up from the water. The moat around the farmhouse was probably dug in place of a wall to keep out cattle, sheep and, more importantly, rabbits from marauding the garden which in the past would have a had a large vegetable patch; it is only relatively recently that most people living in the countryside have given up growing vegetables, but there are now signs of a renaissance as the demand for vegetable seeds is steadily increasing. In her wonderful book *Lark Rise to Candleford*, which is set in the second half of the nineteenth century, Flora Thompson describes how every house in the rural Oxfordshire village had a vegetable garden and that most families also kept a pig. In this part of Hertfordshire there seem to be no livestock at all.

From Moat Farm the path runs between two fields and then hugs the shadows on the edge of a wood before turning a corner next to a smaller pond which had the same layer of bubbling green algae suffocating the surface of the water. From here the path turned black and rutted before reaching a little wood. It must have been about six o'clock. The sun was easing down and the breeze had evaporated completely. The middle-aged woman who was walking her dog smiled and announced that it was the first evening this year that she didn't need her jacket. It was warm, the air was still, holding the drones of occasional cars, and someone somewhere was whistling for their dog. At the end of the wood the land sloped down towards a sunken brook which held a glimpse of the yellow legs of a moorhen picking his way quietly under the edge of the bank; but for the most part the water is tangled up in roots and shade. Shortly after the moorhen, confusion set in. All became clear a couple of hundred yards further on. Almost lost in the hedge was a notice:

> The County Council has become aware of evidence
> that the definitive map of rights of way may be
> incorrect in this area. This will be investigated in
> due course. In the meantime you are invited to
> follow the waymarked alternative route.

In the absence of the waymarked alternative route, I took to following the hedge, hoping that beyond the brow of the field I would stumble across a fluorescent orange arrow. But beyond the brow of the field any semblance of a path gave out and there was nothing but another field. It was thick with wheat, and had tractor tracks running evenly through it. Coming through the trees in the distance was the gleam of a glass roof that appeared to belong to a large greenhouse. The route I had planned led past a nursery so I just headed in that direction.

There is a scene in the film *Gladiator* where the camera follows a hand running through the seed heads of barley, twelve hundred years or so before the zenith of the Roman Empire. King David wrote: 'The valleys also stand so thick with corn, that they shall laugh and sing.' Just three or four weeks ago this field would still have been very much under winter's rule, the wheat would have been muted and lying low on the ground. But what was gaunt is now comely and in every direction there has been a resurrection of leaves, an unfolding of ferns and great swells of blossom. On the seashore the rock pools are filling with prawns, the shallows with shrimps and as the tide comes in against the steep shingle banks it brings with it water that will soon be boiling with mackerel: this is abundance. The moment I stepped into the field I wasn't worried any more about knowing my way; trespassing down the tractor's tracks with wheat up to my hips there was a powerful sense of being released from the dotted lines and a gaunt understanding of joy.

There were definitely a few cars close by but they remained invisible. On the other side of the field ran a much balder tractor track. The ditch next to it must have been dug out quite recently; the imprints of a bulldozer grab were lined up in the mud on the bank and the stumps of young elders and dead lengths of sycamore were strewn along the path. It took a while to work out that the collection of black flashing green feathers lying on the dry mud belonged to a chicken; at first glance I thought it might have been a rook or a carrion crow, and there was more carrion to follow. Rising behind a sickly looking hedge was a small mountain of lettuces – there must have been at least a couple of thousand, with more scattered around the base of this great pile. Inside the glass walls were long neat rows of green seedlings growing in a weedless world. Most of the lettuces that are eaten are cultivated in these optimum environments and they taste of little more than money.

Luckily there was a gate next to the cottages that stood in front of the glasshouses. Under the watchful eye of a dog sitting in one of the cars parked outside one of the cottages

I sat down by the edge of the road and tried to glean some sense from the map, but really the topography didn't match up to the nursery at all. It is always so tempting to settle for supposing – 'I suppose I am here' – and when supposing sets in it tends to fray the certainty of decisions. Banging on one of the doors was an option but there were no signs of life at all, so I headed west down the minor road supposing I might meet someone to ask.

The two cyclists that came peddling down the hill were dressed head to toe in tight clothes, shining helmets and trainers that could have doubled as ballet shoes. For a while they didn't know what road they were on either, so they asked me where I was heading for. 'Oh, Barwick Ford – just follow the road,' I was told. The source of the confusion soon became clear: I had supposed I was at one nursery when in fact on the map I was a couple of inches away, at another. It is strange that nurseries aren't named.

It was still warm, the first real warm evening of the year. The rooks flew slow in the sky and the single trees held still in the fields. The road steepens as it leads through the untidy woods back down to the ford, the crowns of the trees lighting up in the low sun. It could have been the high Corsican mountains or the top of a Cretan gorge, there were just hints in the colour of the bark of the pines, and the spaces in the ground cover but most of all in the deep, dry sunken stream bed that led down next to the road.

I should have crossed the stream before I saw the moorhen, I should have looked more closely at the map rather than merely accepting the polite and considerate notice half buried in the hedge by the County Council: they told me I was lost and I believed them. I am fifty-six and the paths I could have taken are clearer now than they ever have been, but to believe I should have taken them is surely far more of a mistake than any of the choices I made at the time. You see, I cannot be certain the routes I planned have not taken the air out of my life, that I have not chosen the prison of knowing where I am. I cannot be certain that for the most part I have not been heading simply where I have been told to go and that by staying on those paths I have been seeing what I am supposed to see. Yes, I am not meant to be in the middle of wheat fields for sensible and considerate reasons – it is part of the code of the countryside. But then I would not have known the wind stirring the wheat around me and how it sounds like rain.

Barwick Ford, Hertfordshire

Start and finish: OS map 194. Grid reference 388188
Time: four hours

▶ Drive through the farm and over the ford. The farmer very kindly said I could park in the lay-by next to the start of the path. The path is on the left forty yards up from the ford. Follow this path, which is a section of the Harcamlow Way, until you reach a small hamlet.

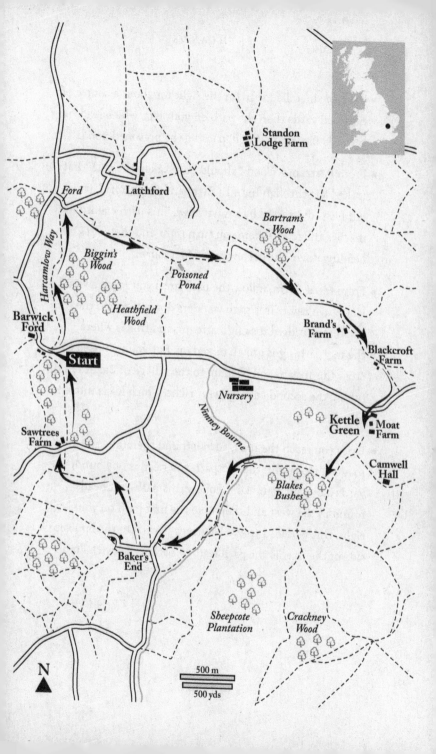

► Take the metalled road on the right for about a couple of hundred yards then the path on your left, which leads up towards Bartram's Wood, passing the poisoned pond.

► From Bartram's Wood I should have taken the path that forked left through Brand's Farm and Blackcroft Farm but I was distracted by a tawny owl. This path eventually reaches the road, where you turn right and then left, heading down the driveway of Moat Farm.

► From Moat Farm, follow the path until you reach a wood. Here turn right. This path wanders down through the wood to a bridge crossing a stream, and this is where the footpath signs are all mixed up. But you will need to cross the stream and head up to the village of Baker's End taking the second path on your right, which leads into the village.

► Once you reach the road, turn left and then take the first road on your right: the footpath you need is one hundred yards along on your right. Follow this path as it heads round to the west and then take the first path on your right: this will lead you to Sawtrees Farm. On the opposite side of the road is the path leading back to Barwick Ford.

The Fifth Quarter

I had never seen a black house: not until yesterday. It looked new, and even the windows seemed to absorb any reflections. It was more like a statement: 'Leave me alone, I want nothing you have to offer – not your charm or your carefully crafted comforting words. I don't need soothing or helping, or roses, and I will not be defeated by love.'

Dungeness has always been alone, separate, isolated. It has been described as the only English desert. The first lighthouse was built in 1615 after a particularly bad storm had claimed the lives of over a thousand men as their creaking little ships were blown, then battered and toppled onto the shifting sandbanks that lie just offshore. But before the lighthouse nobody lived here, because there was nothing to live on. Prior to the lighthouse being built a beacon would be lit at night to warn passing galleons of the sand spit, but all the wood for the flames had to be chopped and brought in: because there are no trees for miles around. I remember seeing it when I was a child running wild on Camber Sands picking up handfuls of Sunset shells. The coast curving eastwards and there on the headland a grey square block blurred in the distance as the heat rose around the fist of a nuclear power station. Even on dead calm days there is the hint of a breeze.

Perhaps this is where the wind waits and rests for a while. I can find no record of where those who manned the Dungeness lifeboat lived but what does remain are accounts of their extraordinary courage in the face of what were always overwhelming odds as they set themselves into the gales and storms and how these regularly took the lives of those who had gone to help others. With the building of a third lighthouse in 1862 came the accommodation for the lighthouse-keepers: a circular structure which looks more like a large hotel mustard pot to house them and their families. This must have been the first time in the history of the place that the sound of children's laughter would have mingled with the wind.

Then in 1883 a railway arrived. A station appeared in a place where nobody lived. There was talk, and plans at the time to create a new port but it never came to anything. But some of those who built the railway bought a few redundant carriages and started using them as holiday homes. I found a black-and-white photograph showing what appeared to be the beginnings of a street, with railway cars and the odd shack laid out in two rows. This too seems to have been rearranged over time by the wind into something that has thankfully no overarching geometry at all. There are, I think, around eighty single-storey dwellings; they are small and they are all different, all personal. Most of them don't have any kind of borders around them: no fences or hedges. The media turn up occasionally and make a fuss about the late film director Derek Jarman's garden but it's not for me, it is a Begonia in the middle of a meadow.

Then in the early 1960s building started on the type A Magnox nuclear power station. It was built right next to the lighthouse, a great grey effigy snorting steam surrounded by high straight fences and dribbling its warm saliva into the sea. But, rather strangely, when you are there it doesn't seem to be as overpowering as it is in the distance, it is so completely unenchanting that you just don't bother to look at it, there is nothing to see; it very quickly becomes invisible. At night I would imagine it might be quite beautiful: many industrial landscapes turn on the charm once the sun goes down, when the noise of the day subsides and the evening air cools and thickens. It is then you can hear them breathing; they come alive with lights and shadows, it is a dark glamour that turns back to dirt in the day.

It is easy to see why Dungeness was chosen as the place to keep this monster in a cage. It is the largest area of shingle in Europe, twelve-and-a-half square miles of stones. Much of it is now out of bounds, cordoned off by lines of red bunting on the Ordnance Survey map and on the ground by a wall of wire, and on the other side of that the rancid remains of war. What was most surreal about the Lydd army ranges was a crumbling two-storey block of flats: it was sacked and empty; with the sun streaming through blocks of coloured glass in the windows it seemed almost as if it was part of an inner-city recreation ground. Having gone through Lydd, I headed south towards Lydd-on-Sea, which is pretty much a mile-long line of small houses facing the English Channel.

Running up against their back gardens are the toy-like tracks of the Romney, Hythe & Dymchurch Railway which begins or ends next to the Victorian lighthouse in Dungeness. The metalled road petered out as I turned westward towards the nuclear power station and on to what appears to be a makeshift track that bends and curves rather curiously in a land where there is nothing to go round. I can't work out whether the track was there before the cottages or the cottages were in place before the track: either way, they appear to have been sown. I once saw a gardener sowing daffodil bulbs. He threw them over his shoulder and planted them wherever they landed, and the buildings here seem to have sprung up in the same manner. There is no symmetry, there hasn't been an architect or a town planner near the place. There is something so completely natural about it, unselfconscious, that this is what might emerge in the absence of planning permission and if when you throw a couple of lighthouses, a nuclear power station and a miniature railway into the mix you end up with something that is utterly memorable, something that hasn't had the hard hand of an ethos placed upon it.

I parked next to the railway station café and wandered in to buy a bottle of water. It was all pies, crisps and sausage rolls inside, it felt sheltered and cared for. Outside, the sky was almost an even white and just about thin enough in places to give a hint of warmth but the breeze had a little ice in it, it wasn't warm enough to sit still in. Just to the north of the café is a little terrace of coastguard cottages, they appeared to be the only buildings that have any sea defences. Just a small row of roofs that have seemingly been built in the middle of an Iron Age fort. It must be odd living there in the midst of this flat expanse but being unable to see any of it from a kitchen window, the embankment completely encircles the houses. From the top of the bank I looked down on a scattering of children's bicycles and washing lines ripe with colour. At some point the sea will break the shingle bank and come galloping over this land. When this happens I would imagine most residents will head for the lighthouses. I couldn't find the path that led from the cottages to the road although it was plain on the map. It had vanished into the shingle.

It always takes time for our senses to adjust. Two hours ago I had been in a green land cradled in trees and soft sloping hills that smelt of earth and cow parsley. Just beyond the cottages is a different-coloured world. There is no earth; the ground is a myriad browns, oranges, greys, ochres and whites. Growing out of these stones are stunted little foxgloves and in patches great yellow stars of prostrate broom, some of them spreading eight feet or more across the shingle. Then in patches the rust-red frills of sheep's sorrel and occasionally little lumps of white flowering sea campion. There was nothing growing above three or four feet.

It was more luck than judgement that took me to a gap in the fence and through a very unromantic kissing gate and across the road to another one. Once through it I was confronted with a sign which read 'Please stay on the waymarked footpath'. Beyond it was a sea of shingle and leading through that was a vague trail where the stones were somehow lighter and every 400 hundred yards or so someone had stood a brick on its end. I assumed this was the path.

The shingle isn't one flat bed, it's slightly undulating as if shaped by the coming and going of the sea, which it must have been. Walking on shingle is not easy; it is sapping. I reckon for every two steps you take you expend the energy of three. The temptation is to veer off the path and walk on the little patches of vegetation where the roots of what is growing there have bound the stones together, making the ground a good deal firmer, but it seemed cruel to trample on what little there is that is managing to eke out an existence. There are in fact 600 native species of plants that grow here, which is a third of all the wild species in Britain, but it doesn't feel that way – even in May everything feels thirsty. After having tramped about a mile and a half the first trees appeared but like the foxgloves they were stunted, grey willows monopolising what must have been an old gravel bed that still had a little water in it.

Grey willows don't appear to have a plan – they just seem to have happened in a manner that untidy hair like mine somehow just finds its own way of being. Much of nature is so beautifully symmetrical. Buttercups, snowflakes, millipedes, nettle leaves, eyes, breasts, wings, feet, sunset shells – there is symmetry everywhere. Maybe this reflects one of the greater laws of physics which have given rise to the shapes of life: that grandeur surely manifests itself just as profoundly in the small as in the vast.

Fifteen minutes beyond the willows I crossed a causeway between two now flooded gravel pits. Here the path turns into a lush line of grass bordered by more grey willow leading down on both sides to the still surface of water and in the middle of these lakes are a few little islands crammed with standing swans and idle cormorants. After the lakes the land turned scrubby; there are gatherings of thistles and the remains of weathered fence posts which didn't seem to bear any relation to each other. I didn't wander down to the main building of the RSPB nature reserve; attached to the outside of a large shed next to the road was a very even row of nest boxes and the thought that there might be chrome chairs and a filter coffee machine somewhere close by really didn't seem that appealing right then. This is a wonderful space to be alone in, if you need to be alone, and I hadn't seen a soul since leaving the coastguard cottages.

There were a few trees on the other side of the road. I had reached pretty much the edge of the shingle, the border where it slides into fields and thousands of sheep. It is more of a bridleway that leads from the road up to a large round storage tank which stands next to a railway crossing. Emperor dragonflies were hurrying over a deep pool on the left of the path. They are perpetually busy; it seems as if they are running errands, taking letters from the sky to the wind. The map shows another large gravel pit but it lay concealed somehow until I reached a hide. I walked in and looked through the narrow glass window out on to what must have been about forty mute swans. They were so unexpected – there had been no hint, no feathers, I heard no calls. The grey willows reflected in the edges of the blue water, the fresh green sedge in the foreground and the splashes of brilliant white, slowly moving swans made a perfect oasis. These were the pure colours of childhood, there appeared to be just one blue, two greens and one white. It's only as I have grown older that I have learned to see beauty in the subtle shades of stones, great grey cliffs and winter – winter is so beautiful now. But apart from the huge yellow stars of prostrate broom and the diminutive foxgloves there is very little of what I know to be May here. May serves up such sensuality, there is nothing brittle in it, everything bends: the land feasts on the rain and the meadows smell of sex and nectar. But there is no blossom here: in a landscape like this one the seasons are a little less loud.

After spending some time admiring a sedge warbler that appeared to have one leg longer than the other I crossed the railway line and started to head across another plain of shingle and back towards the coast.

This is probably the most desolate section of the walk. It was impossible to find the beginning of the path and the lighter-coloured shingle so I just continued in what I thought looked like the right direction, which was vaguely south-east. After about 400 hundred yards a path did appear, two sunken tyre tracks running over the dips and rises. I am not sure it meant to point the way to two yellow triangles and the opening in the fence that led to the path running along the edge of a quarry, but it did. Judging by the surface, very few people had walked this way. Perhaps because they couldn't find it or perhaps because there are few things more ugly than a quarry, they always make me feel ashamed. A friend told me that before his ancestors ploughed the land they cut themselves and let some of their blood drip into the soil in recognition that they were cutting into the breasts of their mother. Looking at the wound on my right it felt like more of an excuse to reassure myself that nature will always find a way to re-colonise, to restore, to reclaim what has been taken.

One of the first plants to set themselves on broken land is ragwort, which is the main food source for the dramatically wonderful crimson pink and black cinnabar moths which took off in flurry under my feet. Ragwort is highly poisonous. The cinnabar moth caterpillars feed on ragwort and the moths that emerge can only be so beautiful and so visible because they have absorbed all that poison. Only cuckoos and nightingales eat them.

I did hear a cuckoo but it must have been some way off. Shingle is predominantly a quieter land. There was the occasional worried oystercatcher raising an alarm and the forlorn whistle from the Romney, Hythe & Dymchurch Railway echoed like a lost seal as the cloud thickened from the east and the air dampened. No one else was walking the pavement which led down to the Pilot Inn. The only signs of human life were one or two passing cars and the occasional flicker of a television, seen coming through the windows of the long line of small houses that runs down from Lydd-on-Sea. The pub though was heaving on the inside, full of families eating an evening meal. I went in to order a lemonade but there was nowhere to sit so I found a table outside and rolled a cigarette. Having absorbed all that emptiness, what I wanted to do was to go down to where the fishing boats had been hauled up on to the shingle next to a collection of oblong shipping containers that had been placed haphazardly at the top of the beach, but instead I headed back along the winding road, and then cut across the shingle and over the little railway line to the car, by the time I reached it it was the only one in the car park. On the way I did visit the Fifth Quarter gift shop, a lair crammed with crystals and dream catchers dripping feathers, with the biggest anchor I have ever seen lying outside the entrance. I asked the woman who appeared from the back whether she felt this was an alternative community, but she didn't really answer me because she didn't want to, I can understand that, because it was none of my business.

Deserts have no truck with pretenders. Bit by bit they strip you down until you either accept what and who you really are or you go mad because of it. All deserts are self-selecting. Once you cross from the fields on to the shingle you are in a completely different template. Here the ideas of what England is just don't fit. They are very powerful ideas: the village, the church tower, the Plough and Harrow, the football team, the cricket team, the Houses of Parliament, Oxford Street, strawberries and cream and lazy summer rivers. That's another country. If you want to go there, the border lies six miles to the north.

Dungeness, Kent

Start and finish: OS map 125. Grid reference 085173

Time: four hours

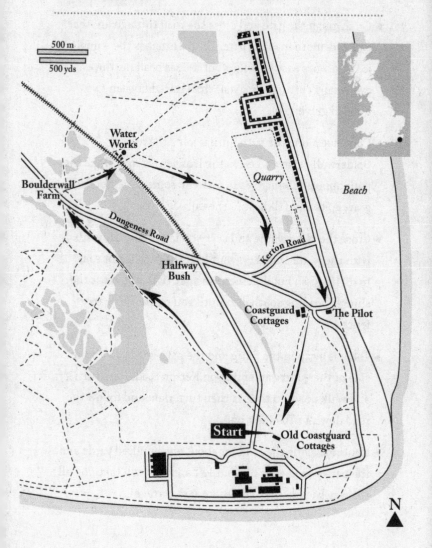

▶ From the Old Coastguard Cottages follow the path northwest until you reach the fence. There is a gap in the fence with a swing gate.

▶ Go through the gate and cross the road through another gap and another swing gate. The path across the shingle is not always easy to follow but it does head northwest, eventually cutting along a narrow track between two flooded gravel pits.

▶ Continue along the path until it joins the road at Bolderwall Farm and cross the Dungeness road. Take the path opposite, which leads between some more flooded gravel pits and follow it to the railway crossing.

▶ Cross the railway line and carry on for about 300 yards with the water works on your left. The path is not easy to distinguish but it is there on your right and cross the shingle heading south east until you reach the quarry fence.

▶ There is a gap in the fence and the path heads down the side of the quarry emerging on Kerton road. Here turn left and walk down to the sea then turn right and follow the road down to The Pilot pub.

▶ Continue along the road for about one hundred yards and the path you need is on your left and this will take you all the way back to the Old Coastguard cottages.

— WALK 3 —

Llandegfedd Reservoir, South Wales

March in May

Reservoirs are too large to hide their sadness. They contain the sorrow of their unwantedness, the water marooned behind a concrete dam waiting to be released. And in the depths, in a half-light, stand leafless trees draped in weed and roofless cottages and barns where trout swim through the windows and pike hover behind doorways. The only weather that looks good on a reservoir is rain. These are places stolen from memories, they sound a perpetual forgetting; these are the places where men and women arrive alone, and they sit in their cars looking out over the water trying to forget what they have been holding back. It wasn't raining here but it wanted to.

Llandegfedd Reservoir was completed in 1965; there are seven or eight buildings that lie under the surface. The valley was dammed where it narrows, south of the village of Glascoed, an incursion of a huge steeply sloping bank of earth which must be covering uncountable tons of concrete. On the map there are two green dotted lines which lead down the reservoir bank; on the ground they don't exist. The dotted line that runs down the centre of the bank is perhaps a remnant of a path that once ran alongside the Sor Brook connecting the village of Llandegveth in the south to Glascoed. And further up on the eastern side of the reservoir are two or three paths that once clearly continued down into the submerged valley, they now just end abruptly at the water's edge. The reservoir is managed by Natural Resources Wales so I left a message on an answer-phone trying to find out why there was simply no indication as to the whereabouts of the footpaths that once led down the reservoir bank.

Unless there is a ruddy great notice expressing a very good reason why the path is no longer in use, I can think of no good reason why – if the path is there on the map – that it should not be walked, so I jumped the gate and headed downwards along the access road leading towards to the pumping station. The ground soon sank into bog and slurry and further on an impenetrable weave of young blackthorn trees sprang from the ground, so I crawled through a hedge and cut round the edge of a field and then back down to the bridge over the brook. The brook flows in a straight still line between two concrete banks; the water is black, and in it moved the ghosts of three large translucent trout. Maybe they were just waiting for the sluices to open and then they would take their chances among the yellowing pools and red-rooted bends that lead downwards from the other side of the bridge into a flickering wood and back into the wild. But by the looks of things they had chosen to stay, they had traded their visibility for a constant supply of food, they looked well fed: they had taken their chances.

On the other side of the bridge, the path runs above the brook and passed along the base of wooded slopes flush with bluebells. Just before reaching the road, where the valley flattens and widens, I met an elderly man who was walking his collie. He told me in a beautifully lilting voice that he only came here to hear the birdsong and that he never walked up as far as the dam. He then pointed upwards into some ash trees and explained that the crowns were dying and that soon the trees would be dead. He was right; in the upper branches the leaves were thinning and blackened and this curse would soon envelop the rest of the tree. There are ninety million ash trees in this country – they account for 5 per cent of all the trees. Ash dieback is now taking hold in the woods near my home in southern England. In three or four years from now most of the ash trees will be dead; they will follow twenty-five million elms into memory. A friend of mine who works with trees said that natural epidemics have occurred throughout history but the causes of this one are very much man-made. He cited the growing global market in trees as one of the major factors in increasing the incidence of this devastating disease and global warming as the reality that fosters it. But it is not just the tree that dies, all the life dependent upon it is also put in peril; trees are mothers to so many other life forms.

The road crosses the brook and the path continues along a rough track that cattle had trodden and mixed into a mire. Yet there were none in the field that opened out from the wood, just a few wiry sheep that cantered over the eastern brow out of sight. Unfolding from the grass in places were rising fronds of bracken and every so often a single bluebell and the sky lightened a little, taking some of the moisture out of the air. There is no real path as such to follow, there are no worn-down areas of grass and the only footprints on the ground belong to sheep and cattle who had quagged the corner of the field forcing me to cut above the path through a little copse, but the stile on the fence line was in good shape. I love these valley fields that slope towards a stream – the balance of trees and grass and another world of moving water.

I knew the path followed the Sor Brook passing Walnut Tree Farm and then down to the village of Llandegveth but it ended in a tall, impassable hedge. Next to it a footbridge led back over the brook and beyond it lay a smaller field with an entrance opening into a wood on the other side. I crossed the bridge but couldn't find a way over the brook; it was running fast and was too deep to wade. The cattle must have heard me: first one cow appeared and ran off; then just before I decided to head for the entrance in the wood, the whole herd came charging through a boggy area, flattening a single-stranded barbed-wire fence, cows and calves mooing loudly, running and bucking with their tails held out behind them as they thundered around a bend in the brook and headed up the field scattering rabbits.

It was very quiet once they had gone and the wood on the other side of the field was damp, the shadows were still. The path runs beyond the stile and from then on tails into a sheep track that jumps a small stream and twists between the trees before reaching a gate. From here I crossed the field and found a tractor track leading which leads up to Granary Farm. It was impossible to find any trace of the path from there which runs from Granary Farm to Glebe Farm so I just set off over the fields heading towards a handful of barn roofs that were showing over the hedges. In the first field a dappled grey horse stood under a large oak. It ambled over to say hello. These horses look as if they are covered in bubbles. I always wonder why a horse should choose to make contact with a human being: is it affection, curiosity or the slim chance of an apple? Perhaps it is all three.

It was food – powdered milk, to be precise – that brought ten or so lambs up to my feet in the field in front of Glebe Farm. They were all different sizes and shapes, a little flock of quislings fed from the hand that also wields the knife. They had no choice but to gang together but they remained clearly separate from all the other sheep. When I sat down two of them lay down next to me and the others gathered themselves around. These were the orphans, the bottle-fed lambs, kept under hot lights, suckled on plastic bottles; some would have lost their mothers, others would not have been acknowledged. Their mothers would have given birth and simply wandered off; some may have been the smallest of a set of triplets and unable to hustle their way past the others to suckle. Sheep are formidable single mothers. They rear their lambs alone; the rams are fathers only in name.

I chose not to walk between a cow and her two calves that were lying almost in a hedge, penned into a thin strip of land by an electric fence. After I had cut round the back of Glebe Farm and headed up the driveway, there was still no sign of a path so the road was the only option. It led downhill past verges crammed with campion and buttercups and after four hundred yards or so I headed left for a little cross on the map, next to it were the words 'Parish room'. The flowerbeds and the polished cars on the other side of the entrance meant that this was now a private house; once upon a time it must have been a chapel. The bluebells were thin and weary, gasping for light on the steep and wooded bank that led down from the house to a brook, where I hoped the path would be – and there it was, along with a few footprints pinched into the mud.

A pint of something would have gone down very well but the Farmers Arms in Llandegveth was shut for the afternoon. Through the windows I glimpsed neatly arranged tables. It must have been the colour scheme that raised the scent of sitting down to eat lunch with my Welsh grandparents: the table mats and the mustard-coloured napkins in plastic rings and how for the most part we ate in a silence that was never uncomfortable. My grandmother was the most gentle woman I have ever known; when I was as a child her hands were always warm and sometimes for reasons I can't remember she would stroke my cheeks and look silently into my eyes, she wouldn't speak yet retained a steady smile as she did this.

An unseen hand had squarely nailed a 'Beware of the bull' sign to the top of a stile on the other side of the footbridge just out of Llandegveth. It should have read 'Beware of the bullocks'. There must have been about seventy of them. At first they seemed unconcerned but when one of them broke ranks and ran towards me, the others then followed. The way back to the stile was cut off by a brown-and-white torrent so I ran up the slope of the field to get the higher ground then turned and yelled, it wasn't a word, it was a battle cry. They stopped about six feet away, by which time we were all breathing heavily; it is strange that one monkey can stop a running river of cattle. The sky was turning to scorn and the breeze had rallied from the east: there can be a merciless side to May. Cold winds that rip and tear the new leaves, scalding and bruising the ones that remain. And sometimes days of rain that hunch the lambs and keep the insects on the ground, leaving the skies empty and the martins and swallows to sit out their hunger.

From the bullock field the path sinks between two high hedges; it is more of a stream bed with grey jutting rocks and handfuls of gravel left on corners and bends. At times the vegetation, the grasses and fronds of determined brambles were so thick it was impossible to see the ground; it felt as if no one had walked this way for quite some time. When the hedges came to an end on the brow above the valley the path opened out next to some farm buildings and what appeared to be a brand new gleaming cattle yard. Rows and rows of metalled stalls, new grey gates ordered and embedded in a cream concrete base. Standing in one of the stalls was a single Friesian cow; there were no others. She looked abandoned but more than anything she was frightened. This is the place where the cattle are gathered before they are taken to market, where they are tested for tuberculosis, but cattle are naturally social and apart from this morning, I hope it was only this morning, this heifer would have been with others she knew. Recently I heard loneliness described as 'barren solitude'. And it is: loneliness is barren. I am not sure that she was even able to lie down.

The cloud base began to descend, blurring the tops of

the valleys and tucking the birds into the hedges except for one raven who was being tormented by three carrion crows. From the cattle yard the path turned to semolina and slurry and smelt vaguely of shit and rats and for about a mile or so it didn't relent. Any firm ground was limited to tiny strips next to a barbed-wire fence and was invariably growing nettles so by the time the fork in the path arrived my socks were caked in mud and my knees burning with nettle stings. The plan had been to walk through a piece of woodland simply called 'The Forest', but the path on the map didn't seem to tally with the path on the ground and what was shown as a large woodland looked in reality more like a copse; so I carried on walking down the boggy track to try to get a better look at the lie of the land. The mud was incessant as I tramped down a line encased between more barbed-wire fences barring access to some solemn fields. The further down I walked, the less inclined I became to go back.

After fifteen more minutes of mud the track reached a corner and some blackthorn trees. On the other side of the fence the ground sank down into what looked like a dry stream bed, it was in fact an abandoned track, a hollow way. It was as if the lights had been turned off inside, it had become a tunnel through hawthorns and blackthorns, a sealed lair that remained darkened in the day; it held nothing other than the intentions of foxes. After about twenty yards or so a window appeared in the thorns and on the other side a green field thick with grass. At the bottom of the valley was a big pink house called Walnut Tree Farm.

It was homely, cared for, with a bending driveway, and

in a paddock at the front of the house was a tall and shining chestnut horse that ambled over to the fence which had a brand new one-plank stile. There was no path on the other side of it, but the footbridge was easy to find, and beyond that the valley rose and became wooded again. It was just a matter of following the brook back towards where I had left it, but there seemed to be no way through a rough field, so I cut up over another stile and followed the edge of the wood uphill until it reached a tumbledown barn nearly hidden by elders and smothered in moss.

Lying on the earth floor in the middle of this windowless space lay the undisturbed skeleton of a sheep. It was impossible to tell how long it had been there, a dead sheep takes little more than six months to decompose completely and in warmer, more humid climates the process is much faster. It just seemed out of place; the barn didn't look used and there was no natural sheep pasture close by. Perhaps it had become imprisoned behind the fence which held in the wood and it seemed from the way it was lying that this was where it had lain down and died. It is not very common to see skeletons of farm animals in the countryside. One of the biggest killers of sheep is bramble thickets; they go in to graze then become snagged and generally die of thirst. Once in a while I see their scattered bones in the midst of brambles.

For the last mile or so I retraced my steps, following the Sor Brook back up to the reservoir. The path is more of a road that runs up on the west side of the pumping station I'd only glimpsed through the trees on the way down. It is a mournful shell of bricks guarded by security cameras and sensor lights bolted on to high metal poles, it is a place that seems impervious to sunshine. At the top of the track I jumped the fence and landed straight on to the road that runs across the wall of the dam. The water in the reservoir was still and grey, the birds had stopped singing.

Natural Resources Wales very kindly returned my call and I ended up speaking to the footpath officer from Monmouthshire County Council. He told me that the council had informed the Ordnance Survey that the footpaths running down from the dam are to be 'extinguished', and the reason for this was to dampen the threat of terrorism around the dam wall. He also went on to say that following a recent survey only 62 per cent of the paths in Monmouthshire are considered to be in good repair and that at some time in the future the management of local paths was to be handed over to local people. There is also going to be a new path running round the entire shore of the reservoir; it will begin and end at the visitor centre, which is now just a skeleton of wood but should be finished sometime soon.

Growing out of the concrete on the dam wall was one little flurry of common vetch. They have miniature pink and purple sweet-pea-shaped flowers. If it was left the seeds would spread and in no time at all this desolate wall would flower. Over the years sycamore seeds would find their way into cracks and along the shores rushes might arrive, bringing sedge warblers and damsel flies. But really the land around the water has been left in pieces and that is the broken reality that has been created. Paths end abruptly and lead nowhere, halves of fields and incongruous hedges, a lake without any trees on the shores. There is a theory that water is incredibly sensitive, that it holds emotions, feelings and memories. If that is the case then the people of Newport are drinking sorrow.

Daniel Morantie is an artist following the visionary tradition. One of his paintings features a woman: he has painted her in profile, she has her eyes closed. The painting is predominantly blues and purples and for a long while I was mesmerised by her grace, not seeing that she was a reflection of the world in which she exists. Behind her in the painting is a reservoir, the dam is constructed of colonnades, with steps leading down to the outflow. And around the shores are trees and buildings that mirror the shapes and contours of a mountainous land. It is beautiful.

Llandegfedd Reservoir, South Wales.

Start and finish: OS map 152. Grid reference 327983
Time: three-and-a-half hours

▶ There is a good place to park just in front of where the path begins. As long as Monmouthshire County Council has not 'extinguished' it, the path leads down from the eastern end of the reservoir. It's a bit scrappy at first but it will continue to lead down to the pumping station, where you will need to cross the bridge and take the path on your right: this follows the stream all the way down to the road.

▶ When you reach the road turn left and then take the path on your right. It is not an obvious path but basically it follows the stream down towards Walnut Tree Farm.

▶ Here things become very confusing because the path simply vanishes; I think it is in the hedge somewhere. But the route I took led me over the footbridge and across the field in front of it, and into the wood on the other side. Here the path peters out. Simply jump the very small stream and head through the brambles to a gate.

▶ Once over the gate, cross the field and you will find a farm track. Follow this track up towards Glebe Farm. From here I followed the road down towards Llangedveth, then took the driveway down towards what was the chapel, and then scrambled down the bank to join the path that leads into Llangedveth.

▶ Once past the Farmers Arms the road bends to the right: the path you need is twenty yards further on the left. Take it. As you head diagonally over the field to your right, you will see a stile. Once over the stile, turn left and follow the very ragged path up to the cattle yard.

▶ Pass the cattle yard, then turn left and continue on this path all the way to the edge of the wood called 'The Forest'. Here I turned left and followed the path down to Walnut Tree Farm.

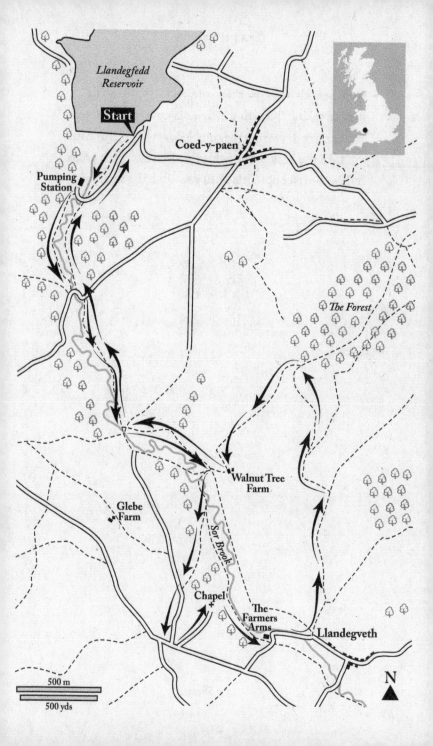

▶ From here clamber over the stile, and then cross the stream, taking the path which leads up to your left and into the wood, passing the tumbledown barn. This path will take you back to the fields that lead along the brook. Follow the river upwards until you reach the reservoir.

Sicklinghall, Yorkshire

What the willows sing

Sicklinghall is made of stout lumps of stone. It has two brown churches and up until a couple of months ago there was one nun living behind the clean windows of the convent ,which is on the opposite side of the road from the pub. She belonged to the order of the Sisters of the Holy Family of Bordeaux, but she has now left to join the remaining nuns in a house in Leeds. On their website is a drawing of Planet Earth with a crack running from the North to the South Pole; above it are the words 'A world to rebuild'.

The convent was the last incarnation of a religious community in Sicklinghall. Since 1852 the village has housed various orders, all of them becoming all but embers before they left the village. What remains is their absence and an unspoken sorrow that they had drifted so far out that no one could rescue them. But the nuns left more than an empty building.

Half way down the main street is what appears to be a walled village green. Apparently when the nuns arrived there were three small dilapidated houses here; the nuns had them pulled down and a small wall was built around the site. Growing on the other side of this the wall is one of the most immaculate vegetable gardens I have ever seen: rows of trimmed peas, leeks in lines, and beyond them potatoes and flourishing cabbages breaking out of a black soil. Whilst this is one season's worth of bounty, it actually takes many years to grow, to learn the intimacies of seeds and soil and, most of all, to welcome in the rain. I had the privilege of meeting the man who tended this garden and if I remember rightly he had been tending that piece of land for well over twenty years. The greatest teachers of patience are surely children and vegetable gardens.

From the vegetable garden the very minor road heading south out of the village passes another unforgettable garden. Standing in front of a 1950s terraced house was a crowd of foxgloves of varying different heights and colours – pinks, yellows, faded orange, whites and crimsons: it was as if the house were in bloom, and that one garden transformed the whole terrace. Beyond the foxgloves the thin road swayed between hedges and fields, and the sun scattered shadows on the grey surface. It is still spring, the white elderflowers are dusted with a cream-coloured pollen and the adult songbirds are beginning to look a little ragged as they hurry through every hour of light to find food for their young. And while the air is warm the ground is still wet and the snails are feasting on everything tender. Just before Sicklinghall House I headed west along a wide yellow-brown path blotched with puddles. A couple of days ago it must have rained heavily and in places the puddles had merged into ponds. To avoid the water those who walked this way regularly had left curving passage ways running through the field of barley which ran up next to the path. But even here the ground was loose and the mud stuck to my boots.

On the other side of the barley field the path runs into a small copse and emerges alongside a vast new willow coppice, it is not surprising that it is not marked on the map. Like hazel, willow grows at an incredible rate, which is why it is a favoured biofuel, but clumped together there is something about it that resembles a field of sugar cane – it is as tall as an elephant. Several years ago I was sitting in the back of a minibus in India. We stopped by the side of the road next to a mountain of chippings and a post-apocalyptic machine gargling smoke and held together with various strands of string and rattling bolts that was somehow pulping sugar cane. We bought misshapen lumps of almost yellow sugar which was wrapped in newspaper and a couple of jam jars of overwhelmingly bitter black molasses. After the haggling had finished, we sat on our haunches drinking chai, and an elderly man with cloudy eyes talked to me about cobras and of how he only slept for one hour every night. In England the field crops rarely rise above a couple of yards, the tallest crop is maize. Yes, there are the hop gardens but they are becoming few and far between. Farmed willow reaches a tropical height; it is less impenetrable than a field of sugar cane but in a light breeze it sounds the same. It was tempting to wander into that dusk, to lose all sense of direction and shake off the hard scales of history; to sit and listen to the teaching of the leaves.

There is at least half a mile of willow and when at times the path lost its tread I was paddling through grass which came up to my knees. I followed the western side of the plantation down to Paddock Farm and cut around past stacks of pallets, bits of machines and broken fence posts; this was clearly where everything was left in case it might come in handy one day. But the bindweed and the morning glory were slowly pulling all of this down into the earth. There must be thousands of tons of metal left on the corners of fields; I have seen tractors completely encased in ivy. There is a combine harvester in an orchard in the Fens which has no paint on it now and there are mice in the engine and grass snakes in the wheels. How this happens is probably down to circumstance and the weather. Just up from where I live an old plough is slowly sinking into the earth on a corner where the path leads to the brow of the Downs. It might have been the end of the day, or it had started to rain heavily, or maybe it had sheared a bolt and the farmer thought 'I'll just leave it there overnight' and something cropped up the next day which became a week which became a year which became a quarter of a century, and there it remains like a name in an old address book.

The clouds were clotting into smaller lumps leaving bigger spaces between them, the sun had some strength in it now, giving fuel to the flies and the racing red admiral butterflies and by the time I reached a eulogy of a dead oak sweat was sliding into my eyes so I took my shirt off and lay down in the long grass for a while. The lapwings who must have been nesting in the barren field behind the oak flew round and round above me calling in worried notes. They do this slowly as if they are almost hovering: I am just as much a predator in their eyes as the carrion crows and the mazed stoats. Despite the catastrophic decline in lapwing numbers over the last forty years it is still, shamefully, legal to take their eggs before 15 April each year. Hopefully somewhere on the ground there would have been little puffs of chicks, which are for a good reason the same colour as the soil and almost impossible to see unless they make a dash for it. It was half a mile or so to the empty spaces of Manor Farm, the tin-roofed barns creaking a little in the rising heat and the occasional flurry of wind spinning the dust up from the surface of the concrete yards. The only signs of life were a few feeding cows their heads peering out from the feeding racks at the base of a vast modern barn the size of a Victorian church.

I am still not quite used to pink elderflowers and their long black leaves; there is a single bush leaning over the wall at Carthick House Farm in Chapel Hill. They seem newly born, still on the breast of creation. I have seen their cream flowering cousins growing out of the flint walls of church towers and among mountains of used car tyres, and sprouting every which way in March, having been cut to smithereens by the metal teeth of industrial hedge trimmers. The pink flowers have less of that intoxicating scent; they are much more demure and not nearly as raunchy. The champagne made from the petals of the pink flowers will sit you down and sing you gently to sleep.

The cream-flowered champagne will deliver you to Bacchus and undo most of your buttons.

Almost clothing another wall running alongside the road was a thick invasion of Himalayan balsam, all the flower heads were a hundred shades of pink and red. I love the way their seeds are jettisoned. I remember fishing one early September afternoon, tucked into the bank, and being lured into the smooth reflections of the upper reaches of the River Eden in Kent and hearing the seedpods cracking open with every light gust of wind. Himalayan balsam seeds are slightly oily and the fish don't eat them as they float downstream to be washed up on another corner. It is strange that the fish leave them alone, because the seeds are delicious, they taste somewhere between hazelnuts and walnuts.

A young girl came skipping down the road eating an ice lolly just before the route takes to the fields again and an elderly couple strolled contentedly arm in arm just beyond the entrance to Wharfe Hill Farm campsite where there was a glimpse of a small shop and some tables and chairs, but there was no one else around once the tarmac had turned to earth. The path across the fields leading to Swindon Farm had been ploughed up and the field was crammed with oilseed rape – and wading through ripening rape fields is not at all easy. So I bumped along the hedge and followed an overgrown line between the set-aside and some rape and after a contretemps with a thousand thistles found the bridge over Baffle Beck. On the other side the grass was shining and the path ran easily past the back garden of the farm bright with swings and along the edge of a field of sea-green oats. The cereal crops are just beginning to turn, their lower leaves are now edged in yellow, and in the evenings the barley can seem almost blue.

Lying in the middle of a soft-grassed meadow beyond the oats a hare crouched and flattened with his ears stroked onto his shoulders. I read once that Romanies would walk in ever decreasing circles around a hare stranded in the middle of a field and the author stated that in most cases they usually got close enough to fall on the hare and take it home for the pot. I just wanted a closer look – they are such beautiful creatures. After six circles I must have been within ten feet of it and on the point of realising that by now it must be frightened – when suddenly it took off and vanished into the skirts of oats.

The geese too were out of sight, disagreeing somewhere around a large pond that lies hidden behind some trees just before the path turns at ninety degrees and heads north in pretty much a straight line to Kirkby Overblow. The village juts out between trees on the brow of an escarpment; a brown church tower and various roofs and windows flashed in the sunlight, which by now was almost unbroken. Warm June days have a natural ease, the cows drooling in meadows and the trees sleeping in the heat. In the index of my road atlas there are twenty-one Kirkbys. The name simply means 'settlement by a church', and Overblow is an evolution of Oreblow, indicating that this was a place where iron was traditionally smelted. It is rare to find a path between villages that takes a straight line – most of them meander and veer along the lie of the land. At a time when most people simply walked from A to B paths were trodden around the easiest places to cross the stream and the most consistently dry land to travel over.

Many of the footpaths in this land are thousands of years old.

Instead of stiles the farmer had installed new metal gates. Set within each gate is a smaller one, a gate within a gate. I had never seen ones like them before. There was a simple elegance to these gates and they opened onto large fields where the grass was being eaten down to the ground by a relaxed herd of milking Friesians. As the land sloped down towards Baffle Beck again a familiar piercing call rose above the sweet-stemmed meadow on the other side of a barbed-wire fence. Just to make sure, I skinned the fence and quietly eased through the grass to get a glimpse of a nesting pair of curlew. They are summer residents here, they fly in to dance and breed above a line that runs north of Birmingham, but I have never seen them inland before: for me they are associated with the coast, their footprints snaking across mudflats and their slim, curved bills held out before them in flight. They are such plump birds and like other waders seem utterly uninterested in human beings. In their eyes I am a Gweilo, a white ghost, a purveyor of grief, and the pact they have made with the redshanks, the dunlin and the sandpipers is to ignore me completely.

The herd of young bullocks holed up in the last field before Kirkby Overblow took a different view. It was impossible to enter the field, as what must have been about thirty of them crowded around the stile accompanied by half the flies in England – they were definitely up for a party. No amount of reasoning or posturing persuaded them to move and they trailed me down the fence line, their energy palpable. I have sensed this before: they were excited. The field grass was not peppered with cowpats, it was new and uneaten and they were young bullocks and by the look of the grass they had just been given the field. Perhaps only just this morning they would have been cooped up in the half-light of a barn and fed according to the clock. Now they had sunlight on their backs, fresh food whenever they wanted and fifty times as much space as they had been used to. This same energy of excitement is present when house martins gather together on the church roof in my home village, thousands of them, before they take off back to the southern Sahara. It is there when male and female winged ants emerge all at once from their underground cities, the whole colony coming up into the light. And once they have flown, the crowds of worker ants slope back into the earth. But thirty or so very excited young bullocks need to be given a wide berth. So the only option was to walk round the field and re-join the path which darkens and narrows between the limits of gardens before opening into the light when it reaches the road that runs through Kirkby Overblow. There was no one else in the pub and not one car passed by as I sank a pint of ginger beer on a small terrace overlooking the land rolling southwards.

To begin with, the track leading back to Sicklinghall was true to its name. Marsh Lane was a blend of mud and eager brambles, a tumbledown wall on one side and a line of high blackthorn bushes on the other. The young man driving the tractor must have been no more than seventeen. He was tearing up and down the field beyond the wall turning hay and had one of those sweet faces where you can see the features of the man beginning to set in the face of the boy. As I walked

— 47 —

down the path towards Lund Head the mud turned to pebbles and the blackthorn gave way to hazel, fraying the sunlight into small fish swimming through the stones. I love the way tunnelled paths within woods open into fields, doorways between one world and another: how within two steps the smell of the air changes. Woods are cooler in summer and warmer in winter. The field at the bottom of the valley held the heat. On the other side of an overgrown brook is a wide verge with newly planted trees and between them the dazed wanderings of meadow brown butterflies.

It isn't so far back along the road into Sicklinghall, where the primary school was finishing for the day and mainly mothers had gathered in small groups, some of them half bent listening to their excited children spilling stories. I must have heard the words 'ice cream' about six times as I strolled past. In ten minutes' time the gate will be quiet and three hours from now the meadow browns will be heading into the grass and closing their wings. As dusk sets in, the hare will find somewhere safe to sleep; they tend not to have burrows. The badgers will come up from their setts. The young cubs will play for half an hour or so before their parents take them hunting. And in a room somewhere in Leeds an elderly nun will be saying her prayers, running the rosary through her fingers knowing the scent and the sounds she left behind her in the unstirred air of an empty mansion.

Sicklinghall, Yorkshire

Start and finish: OS map 289. Grid reference 356385
Time: four hours

- There is a good car park in Sicklinghall next to a very good little shop. From the car park, head down to the road and turn left. Carry on until you reach the small enclosed vegetable garden, and here turn right.

- Carry on down this minor road until just before you reach the entrance to Sicklinghall House, where you take the path on your right. This path runs pretty straight to a minor road: here turn left.

- Paddock House Farm is about half a mile down this road and here take the path on your right, following it all the way to Manor Farm.

- At Manor Farm turn left and take the minor road on your right. This road winds down to Chapel Hill and doubles back on itself, leading down towards the caravan park.

- Once past the caravan park, the path joins what is effectively a ninety-degree turn in the road. Follow this path, and take the first path on your right leading towards Swindon Farm. The footbridge is half buried in the bushes running along the field boundary. Once over it, the path leads along the back of Swindon Farm.

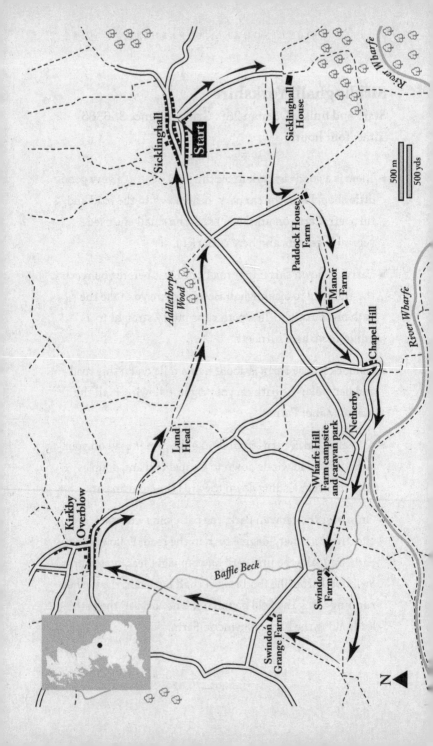

▶ Follow it for about a mile and then take the path heading towards Kirkby Overblow, which you will be able to see in the distance. Follow this path all the way up into the village.

▶ Walk through the village and then take the path on your left, which runs down past Lund Head and then on to the bottom of the valley and up, passing Addlethorpe Wood on your left.

▶ Once past the wood turn right on to the bridleway. This leads to the road, where you turn left and head back into Sicklinghall.

Crumpsbrook, Shropshire

The radar islands

The white thistle was being bumped by the wind. I bent down and felt the leaves just to make sure they were as sharp as kitten's teeth and that this really was a thistle stem that just happened to have produced a white flower. Many more of them were flowering on the slopes leading up to the top of a hill that seems to have been created entirely by human hands.

The forecast had said rain in the afternoon but the lustre leaching through the white sky dispelled any idea of it. Just before the village of Crumpsbrook the road crosses a cattle grid, and on the other side of the cattle grid is a hand-painted notice telling you the land you are now entering is under the jurisdiction of the 'Clee Hill Commoners Association'. The black-painted letters were fading and the edges of the sign were rusting. Common land has a very different feel to private land; it tends to be the land on the edge, the land that won't take the plough, the parcel the landlord could afford to be generous with, which is the meanest gift of all. But these lands of bracken and tough heather, what used to lie at the edge, have now revealed themselves as the true oases they always were. Apart from the National Parks, common lands are among the few remaining places where you can just wander. Nothing here is even, there are lumps everywhere; there is no symmetry for the eyes to rest on as the land leans upwards onto Clee Hill and the tops of the uneven masts rise from the summit of Titterstone, which lies to the north.

In the absence of a car park, I left the car in what was barely a lay-by opposite the first house in Crumpsbrook. As I was putting my pack together the postwoman turned up. She didn't know of a car park either, but said it would be fine to leave the car here for a while. The path was nearly invisible, a semblance of a way that in winter would have been pretty much impassable with its black pools of water held in round, deep dips. It staggered north over the dark green and brown unfenced land before crossing another minor road where a man lay asleep in the front seat of a white van. On the other side of the road lay a grey straight line leading up towards Magpie Hill. In places the white thistles outnumbered the purple. They are marsh thistles – not that the ground was wet – and are just as ragged and sturdy as their purple sisters, but they sing a different song. There is something of another world about them, as if they should be growing on Saturn, and if you peeled the hard spiny casing off the stem and ate the tender fruit inside, on Saturn you would remain for ever more. A pearl-bordered fritillary was being tumbled over the land; its wings were not strong enough to cope with the wind that would suddenly ambush the steady breeze. It almost lay down in the rough grass in front of me; the undersides of its wings are marked with an indecipherable code of splashes, half-moons, outlines and dots. The lower wings seem slightly more fluent and in the sunshine apparently have the same sheen as mother-of-pearl. There were other butterflies as well, posses of meadow browns, ringlets and red admirals. There would be no pesticides used on this land, not that any of these butterflies could ever be described as pests; and sadly I have seen them dying in their dozens on verges next to where the fields have been recently sprayed. There is something here that was once active: their land reeks of a past endeavour.

I had to climb Magpie Hill. This wasn't planned: it was the shape of the path winding and narrowing upwards into the increasing intensity of the wind. It didn't arrive at the top; it veered west and levelled out through a cutting. At the end stood a roofless brick shed, inside every inch of the ground was covered in sheep shit. The west wall was missing and beyond lay these vast grey vertical slabs of concrete built into the side of the hill; they looked as if they might have been left behind on the moon, these the visible remains of endeavour. The greater part of what has now been left behind up here runs in shafts and tunnels, as all of this hill has been mined: firstly for coal and now for dolerite, which is used in drainage channels and road construction. The last of the miners walked off the hill at the end of the Second World War but men had been punching out the rock and coal here for well over 400 years. There is no greater oblivion than the solid darkness of a mineshaft. The men who worked Clee Hill, who dug the shafts and picked out the underground seams, were as physically hard as the blackstone they found. What they have left are craters and mounds and a village of empty red-brick sheds which over time are becoming the stones of an abandoned land.

A deep moss had smothered a large crater which sunk in front of another empty red-brick shed standing next to what looked like a young hornbeam, and beyond it a couple of roof tops leant up above the ridge. I followed a sheep track onto the brow of the hill where the land flattens and becomes a moor. The sound of chains and the echoes of hammers and engines dragged through the air and in the distance to the west the vague shapes of quarry trucks laboured slowly over a grey and treeless wound; this is the one working quarry left on the hill.

There isn't really a need for paths here, not when the air is clear. In winter there must be days when this land is locked in fog, when the distance is lost as the cloud base sinks below one thousand feet. But the birds are nesting now; the skylarks and meadow pipits who have sung ceaselessly since I left the car have threaded grasses into small bowls which they have hidden in the tents and tufts of grass and they deserve to be undisturbed. When mining was at its height here, men would have walked in from Knowbury, Doddington, Hopton Bank, and some from further afield, the moor is sown with trails. It is now impossible to know whether the sheep are using the trails the men created or men followed the trails trodden into the hill by sheep and cattle.

There didn't seem to be a great many livestock around

Random Cottage. Once it must have been a high farm, as the land around it breaks into small fenced fields that stand alone in the middle of the moor. Swimming on the pond some way in front of the cottage were six white geese and around the edges of the pond swayed clumps of yellow iris in full flower. These ponds and pools in the middle of moors tend to be the colour of night. Some of them surely still hold offerings of gold and silver unfolded into the water by our forebears to wrench a favour from the gods of fertility and healing. There can be something quite sombre about these pools, but this one grinned and flashed straight off the page of a colouring book. Maybe this is all the gods desire.

The dogs – and there must have been about twelve of them – wanted attention. They were holed up behind a metal-gauzed gate in one of the yards of Random Cottage, barking and wagging their tails and several of them had jumped up resting their front paws on the top bar. But the sky was beginning to bruise and Titterstone Hill now loomed up in front of me. The slopes of the inner crater look as if they were made on the moon and above them on a large plinth stands a giant golf ball, and to the right of it a flat-roofed bluish building that clearly emerged from the same mould as a 1960s secondary modern. It is a classic lair, the castle of a brilliant villain who collects whispers and distils them into fearful forms. All that was lacking were some palm trees, a helipad, a swimming pool and a couple of men wearing expensive suits standing before a large wrought-iron gate with their hands clasped in front of their testicles. I am sure there is a gate – I could see bits of a road winding upwards – but even from a distance the building looks as if it has been recently raised from the bottom of an ocean; the wind and rains are slowly consuming it. As testament to the rain and bulging out of the grass on the way to the base of the crater are large pillows of moss, several of them hosting stars of white flowers. The wind was lighter here as the land is protected by the hillocks on either side, and when the sun crept through a gap in the clouds I lay down and took some water and watched the heads of grasses against the sky.

There is a path leading in from the east that runs up Titterstone Clee Hill. On the map it looks as if it follows part of the now disused railway that once carried stone and coal from the top down into the valley. Approaching from the south, there is an unmarked path that rises very steeply and runs up a gully, arriving at another broken shed on the other side of the dishevelled road that leads up to the lair. From here I clambered up on to a bluff behind the shed: I shouldn't have done it but the view of the crater from there is worth all the extra heartbeats of the sheep track down, which wobbles above a flooded mine shaft. There is an elegance about the crater: sloping weathered lines of yellow grey rock give the impression that it is in the process of melting. There is not a single tree, and what grass there is in the flat base of the bowl appears to be thin – just about hanging on; but, most important of all, it is big enough to be small in.

There is something about the edge of the desert here, where what little that grows is at the edge of endurance. The British Isles has very few of these places, where the land exists almost beyond the limits of vegetation – the ridges and summits of the Black Cuillins on the Isle of Skye, the peaks of Tryfan and Yr Wyddfa in North Wales and a few lonely, rocky lumps battered by the sea off the Cornish coast. In these places you are walking on the surface of Titan or the moon and, as the Desert Fathers discovered, in the absence of life the intensities and the vulnerabilities of existence are heightened.

It was impossible to know how deep the flooded mine shaft is; the water is clear around the edges but oblique from there on in. I took a sheep path running up the side of the crater and re-joined the main path, which is relatively well trodden to the summit which lies beyond the radar golf ball ticking away, quietly monitoring all the air traffic within a hundred-mile radius. On the summit there is a concrete trig point and just beneath it a small circular roofless dry stone shelter, more of a windbreak than anything else, which would be utterly unable to offer any protection from the closely packed pencil lines of rain slanting out of the clouds to the north, east and west; Titterstone Clee Hill was being besieged. To the south-west the humpbacks of the Malvern Hills were clearly visible, and on a clear day it is possible to see the summit of Cader Idris rising far in the distant west. To the north lie the blue and green Shropshire Hills and the steady outline of Long Mynd fading fast into the rain. But it was the Shropshire Hills that looked so enchanted, a separate kingdom, a prelude to the much wilder land lying to the north. The wind started to flurry and bluster as it does before the arrival of rain, a thousand feet below, the surface of the land turned fluid, flooded by a sea of travelling shadows. In the scheme of things 1,749 feet isn't high, it is still a hill; in the British Isles it is only land above 2,000 feet that is classified as a mountain. I am not sure whether hills have summits or whether they just have 'tops', but the top of Titterstone Clee Hill feels like a summit. It isn't high enough for us to experience what mountaineers describe as 'the beckoning silence' that all the higher mountains hold, but it is just high enough to be above the noise of cars, drills, drum and bass and lawnmowers. It is a process and a desire: you pack, you walk and you climb out of that world.

Somewhere in a world of grey scree gathered on the eastern side of the hill a wheatear had hidden her nest. I didn't mean to disturb her – she emerged out of the stones and scolded me loudly. Below her a troop of walkers were making their way upwards, they were the first people I had seen since the man asleep in the car. They must have been in their late sixties and early seventies; a small group of men dressed in khaki trousers and checked shirts led the way, followed by a group of women and lastly a lone man who was taking it step by step, stone by stone. I love the way older men automatically impart knowledge. Having given me a tour of the horizon they then told me it was going to rain and that there were a couple of old barns near the path at the bottom of the hill that leads through the bracken to Cleeton, should I need some shelter. From the base of the hill I looked back and saw them turn thin and trickle into the sky and they were right about the barns: the buildings were small and empty, not big enough now for the amount of hay needed to fill the stomachs of the numbers of wintering cattle that make keeping them economically viable. Many of these outlying barns now lie empty; they tend to be too far off the beaten track to be converted to houses and most of them are slowly and simply becoming derelict.

It is about a mile through the bracken to the road which slips down into a small wooded valley and over a deep beck before rising steeply into Cleeton, passing the small brown church of Saint Mary. It was open. Inside, a table was laid with biscuits, packets of crisps, a kettle, some tea and coffee and cartons of drink. The prices were handwritten on a piece of white card; in the absence of a pub it was an act of kindness: they weren't making money, they were providing sanctuary, especially in winter, for all those walking down off the hill. Sitting in the porch, munching a few biscuits, I watched as the flat slabs of path stone began to stipple; it was hardly a shower, more of a sprinkle. The hedge running up next to the road must have been as old as the church: it was made up of hawthorn, dog rose, elder, honeysuckle, blackthorn and holly. There is a rule of thumb that says that a one-stock hedge will gain an extra shrub every hundred years. I love the way the natural world is inclined towards diversity: how on shingle beaches it is almost impossible to find two matching stones, that no two oak trees are the same, and that each pair of house martins builds a differently shaped nest. I think it was Satish Kumar who recently said that diversity is the signature of the richness of the natural world.

The foxgloves growing along the edge of the Jack Mytton Way leading back towards Crumpsbrook were all different shapes and sizes, some of them were well over eight feet tall. In places they lined the side of the track. I have never seen so many of them out in the open – usually they are standing sentry just inside the boundaries of woods; they look tropical on open land. The Jack Mytton Way runs ninety-three miles from Bridgnorth to Much Wenlock and was named after a man who had the notable distinction of being expelled from both Eton and Harrow public schools. He was an MP for about fifteen minutes and died at the age of thirty-eight in a debtors' prison, having drunk and gambled away his family's fortune, much of which would have been amassed from the rents squeezed from the knuckles of the men who mined and worked this land. These hills belong to them; they have dript their sweat into the soil, they have dug and pickaxed their names into these slopes which now feel released from an aching toil. One hundred years ago these hills would have resounded to the noise of engines, spades and voices, the rasp of metal on stone, they are now quiet again. Up on the top of Titterstone Clee Hill we are just far enough above the noise we all make to be released from it.

Crumpsbrook, Shropshire

Start and finish: OS map 203. Grid reference 627783
Time: four hours

- There isn't really any parking in Crumpsbrook but there are odd little lay-bys, so I left the car in one of them, just in front of the telephone box.

- From Crumpsbrook follow the minor road south, with Catherton Common on your right. Just before you reach a left-hand turn in the road, take the path across the Common on your right. This heads over the Common, then cross another minor road: Craven Cottages are on your right.

▶ From here I walked up the side of Magpie Hill and found the track that runs past all the old mine buildings. I carried on until I could see the roofs of a couple of cottages in front of me, then headed right up on to the ridge and over the moor towards Random Cottage.

▶ At the pond, turn left and follow the bridle track along, with a few very small fields on your right. Then head up north, passing Random Cottages. Here, I kept going along old mine tracks until I reached the base of Titterstone Clee Hill and cut up along a small path, which heads up towards the ridge. Keep going until you reach the summit.

▶ From the summit the path heads down, passing a long section of scree on the left and then on down into the valley, arriving just in front of Callowgate Farm. From here turn right and follow the path all the way into Cleeton St Mary.

▶ Head up the hill, walking out of the village, and the Jack Mytton Way is on your left. Follow it and take the second path on your right, which leads down along the edge of a wood. This path will take you back into Crumpsbrook.

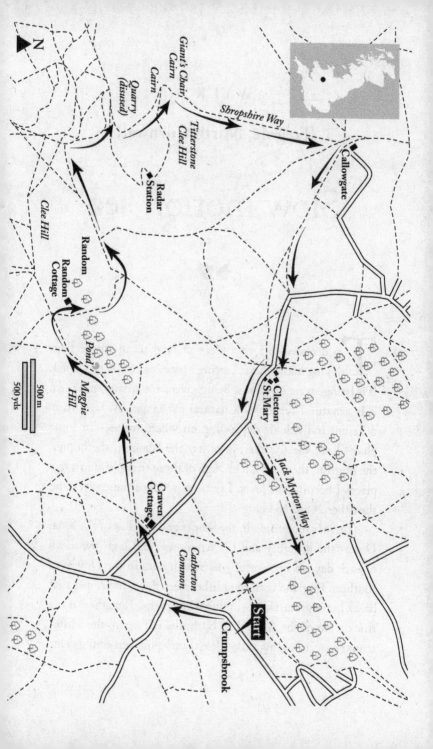

Tregole, North Cornwall

Slow motion sea

To declare we love a piece of land means more than loving being there. Loving a piece of land is relational. It is being aware of what is being given, and giving in return; it is a natural response, a natural exchange. We are many different individuals depending on where we are. In some places I am the traveller, in others the labourer, the hunter, the pilgrim, there are not enough of those times. But in a few places I become the lover. Lovers experience themselves and the other as sacred beings.

There is something in the shapes and the dust of the Sinai Desert the brutality and the tenderness and how the dawn of each day feels powerfully new; as it does in the Downs of southern England with their lithe, steep flowering slopes that break into the sea, their winding white paths. Then there is the thick scent of the Australian bush: the red earth, the white-trunked trees holding yellow leaves up against an endless blue sky, how the sunlight echoes from the eucalyptus leaves and drips onto the ground. And the summer light that I drank in as a child, that nursed me: I have constantly looked for it always and have not found it anywhere on earth other than Cornwall. It arrives in mid-June and leaves towards the end of September and it is at its most vivid when the wheat and barley stand ripe in the fields.

There are no footpaths to Bastard Mill. On my map, the name was written above the confluence of two streams that meet and swing down a wooded valley, emerging on the beach at Millook. Here the land drops between the wild cliffs running from Widemouth bay to Crackington Haven in North Cornwall. The high-banked hedges holding in the road to Tregole, where the walk begins and ends, were crammed with flowers – toadflax, honeysuckle, meadowsweet and great long spikes of purple loosestrife; there were no bare patches, every square inch was alive. This fecundity is fermented by warm air and rain delivered by the Gulf Stream. In winter Cornwall can be testing, it can rain for weeks on end; and even in the summer the wooded paths never really dry out. But by June, when the first bulge in the Azores' anticyclone usually reaches Cornwall, the winds relent and the summer light arrives, throwing the clocks and – for a while at least – lifting the sentence of time.

After ten minutes or so of wandering up and down a delightful bridleway leading from where I had parked the car in the hamlet of Tregole it became clear that the footpath to Trewint was not marked, so I clambered over a gate and headed off in the direction of some rooftops jutting above the trees.

What looked as if it might be a twenty-minute stroll took an hour. The first field had recently been cropped by cattle but on the other side a stream had eaten a ten-foot gully into the earth. It wasn't possible to jump it and, whilst it was not impossible to climb into it, there was no guarantee of my being able to climb out again. So I followed the stream valley upward.

The only way out of the field was over a barbed-wire fence and down into a seven-foot gulley. The stones on the stream bed were more slippery than polished ice and, after ten yards and a couple of wobbles when some oak roots appeared, I hauled myself up into a bramble patch and skinned the barbed wire fence down into the uncut meadow on the other side. In the shade along the edge of the field the grass was still heavy with dew, but out in the open the mid-morning sun was drying the stems and rousing the butterflies.

As I followed the land upwards the gully eased. Halfway up the meadow some cattle had trodden a way down so that they could drink from the slow stream. I pulled myself up into a copse where the earth was leaching water into boggy pools and the air smelt of old coats and peppermint. At the edge of the copse the lower branches opened into another meadow; there was no fence marking the boundary, the copse simply became the field. It was still and muggy; the remains of mist occasionally floating over, thickening the sunlight into chambers and rooms

At the top of the field the obstacle was vertical: a hefty dry stone wall topped with nettles and hawthorns, but luckily sheep had recently blazed a trail onto the top and from there it was a straightforward leap into the long grass.

Middle Trewint stood at the end of a narrow metalled road; it was more of a driveway. The map was clear about the fact that the non-existent path ran around the back of these two coastal cottages, but finding a way round would mean a good deal more cross-country walking. Just before I started doubling back a man appeared at the door of one of the cottages; he had a tousled head of greying hair and was in conversation with his mobile phone. He rang off and told me his name was Anthony, and that he had moved in five years ago with his family and was renting the cottage from a local farmer. He thought the path ran through his next-door neighbour's garden and very kindly led me round the back of his cottage, past a bed of onions growing in a sheltered spot just outside the back door. Onions are one of the few vegetables that will tolerate the salt spray blown up the valley off the sea during the storms. The rest of his vegetable garden was growing in a polytunnel behind the cottage.

I live some six miles from the sea in the lee of the South Downs and even here I have seen beech and hawthorn trees completely rusted by sea spray that has made its way over Firle Beacon and into the valleys on the north side of the Downs. Behind Anthony's house is an old disused track that now runs through a tunnel of blackthorns; it is still wide enough for a cart but couldn't take a tractor. As it enters Millook Water valley it curves into a wood. Anthony had said he'd heard of a path that followed Millook Water from the head of the valley and joined the main path leading up from the sea. He had some friends living in an intentional community nearby and they occasionally walked that way.

The path had recently been made clear by cattle; a handful of them had broken into the woods and must have made a dash for it along a narrow line swaying between nettles and brambles now torn and swollen with hoof prints. It didn't matter. Come what may the stream ran to the sea, all I had to do was follow it through temples of trees.

For a while the path slid along the edge of the stream through a world of floating pools of light and damper tunnels of shade. Five hundred yards further on the cattle had headed up the stream bed of another tributary and from there on in the path was less distinct. Occasionally it would enter open areas where nothing was growing on what was a carpet of soft brown leaf litter and then on, over and around collections of small mounds.

I don't know how long I had been walking when I arrived beneath a clump of ancient beech trees and it was only when I sat down to take some water that I realised I had completely forgotten to find Bastard Mill; Anthony had said it was little more than a pile of stones now. Maps have one disadvantage, and that is the need to constantly refer to them. The beauty of following a stream to the sea is that you can be where you are without having to know where you are. It becomes almost a meditation, a relinquishing of all thought – the tight wires of worries, the vanity of plans, these evaporate, leaving only the purity of what is seen and heard in the present moment.

Nothing was growing under the beech trees apart from one sallow holly. The water flowing over the stones in the stream was largely silent and what I thought was a falling leaf turned out to be a white butterfly. Occasionally all the wood pigeons would sing at once, and then it was quiet again. From the beech trees the narrow path rose high above the stream, teetering along the side of a steep slope, with the vague edges of open areas coming in and out of focus through the trees on the other side of the bank. Again I lost track of time and only came to as the path headed down into a clearing. The grass on the verges had been recently strimmed and a bridge led over the stream. This was the beginning of the waymarked path to the sea.

Here the stream widened slightly and stilled every so often into deep pools. Small fish create small ripples. The trout that were nudging the surface here must be small, wily and strong, surviving the torrents that would run off the valley and fill the stream following a storm. But there wasn't a hint of rain, the woods smelt of mulch and ferns, and the warm air blurred in the windows of sunlight where flies tangled and span.

After about a quarter of a mile the path arrived at some hidden houses and from there climbed over a high stile between two young oak trees that had been planted either side of it. The common blue butterflies in the meadow on the other side of the stile were in a hurry – when the sun is shining they live life at full speed. Once just up the coast from here I woke up early in the morning in a cottage right next to a cove in north Devon. Behind the cottage was a large field and I went out to gather a few blackberries for breakfast. It is the only time I have seen common blues still. They had settled in their dozens in the hedgerows, all of them with their wings open taking in the first heat of the day. The British blue butterflies are small in comparison with some of their Asian cousins but a mile of sky is condensed into their one-inch wings. The male and female damselflies further on seemed to be taking some time out from one another; the glistening blue males had gathered around some rushes that were standing at the beginning of a long field where the path really becomes a bridleway. Further on the tourmaline green females were picking their way over the tops of some flowering bramble bushes; I am not sure how far the space was between them. At the end of the field the wood gradually thins. Through the leaves the embroidered side of a treeless slope appeared and as I wandered along, passing an empty garage, the sky opened. The change in the air was immediate: within a couple of inches the scent skewed from horses to fish. In the window of a cottage stood a carved and hand-painted herring gull and not so far away from there on the other side of a five-bar gate is the sea.

The even curve of Millook beach is enclosed by cliffs and backs into the land only where the stream reaches the sea, the water disappearing beneath smooth grey pebbles and running out over a line of slippery green weed. The sea was restless, hustling determined medium waves through a forest of rocks onto the shore. Five minutes after arriving the only other three people – a father and his two young children – left and when they had gone I had the stones to myself. I lay down and watched several planes 30,000 feet up flying out over the Atlantic to Los Angeles, Florida and the Caribbean postcards of leaning palm trees, white sands and azure blue waters. It's the ubiquitous picture of paradise stuck to the glass in the travel agents' windows from Penzance to Prague. Here the sea flashed between greens and blues, the white water turning brilliant as it rolled in and the gulls yelled their anthem into an empty sky.

Just up from the beach is a handwritten notice explaining that sea bass do not breed until they are over seventeen inches long. Underneath the writing was a seventeen-inch-long line arrowed at either end: it replaced a similar sign that stood next to it which the weather had rendered pretty much unreadable. From here the South West Coast Path heads steeply upward through gorse, heather and thrift. Gabriella and Gernhart were walking down, two German women who were heading for Crackington Haven. They explained that they walked a bit of the coast path every year; they smiled continuously and were travelling light, their packs were small; I didn't ask how long they had been walking for but their faces were brown and their hair windswept. The view from Bridwell Point at the top of the cliff extends as far as the radar station in Morwenstow, over nine miles of waves that were breaking some 300 yards out and moving in slow motion towards the land. The coast path runs along the road as it heads down to Widemouth. I did try the small green dotted line on the map that leads along the cliffs but it was impassable so skinning the fence was the only option. On the other side a clump of brambles hid the ditch that I fell into, the thorns cutting red bleeding lines from my shorts to my armpit. I had dispensed with the shirt long before I reached the sea.

I pulled my shirt back on again before going into the bar of the Widemouth Manor Hotel. It was quiet but the barmaid told me that in the evenings half of Bude left the town and came here to eat. The garden has a large mown lawn and is full of flowers; in the centre stands a hollow plastic brown tree with a slide emerging from the top of it. Next to it is a very small red and blue elephant on metal springs. The main attraction was surely the bouncy castle but there was only one girl jumping up and down inside it and she retreated when two small boys arrived and started throwing themselves against the walls and doing somersaults.

As I left I could hear them planning to climb out on to the roof, and some way back down the road a distant voice shouted, 'Come down from there.'

Down from the hotel, the path runs along the metalled entrance to the John Fowler holiday village, an organised enclave of chalets, pathways and signposts. Some white wooden railings led up the walkway to the sales office, which was a neat and tidy Portakabin where the sales assistant explained that the footpath continues round to the right of the entrance. It runs between some high hedges where a small white, grey and black striped bird was resting in some blackthorn branches above a gate; it was finch-like, and seemed quite at ease but slightly out of place. Maybe it had been blown in across the Atlantic. I have never seen a bird like it before and have checked all the bird books in the house but what it is and where it is from remains a mystery.

There is clearly somebody living in the ramshackle couple of caravans that are snugged behind a gate further on up the track. The doors and shelves of a caravan kitchen unit were spread out for sale in front of a fenced enclave. It felt as if this was the home of a single man who had almost hidden himself from view, a hermit. I would love to have met him but he wasn't there. From here the path becomes as wide as a drove and heads up onto the brow of a small hill where it meets a gate then shrinks and narrows into a breeze-less alleyway between two high, overgrown stone walls. Handfuls of shining blackberries hung down, and there were great banks of pink-and-white bramble flowers and bursts of yellow and green toadflax. The path was muddy in places, the conversation of a thousand wings filling the air – bees, wasps, hoverflies, flesh flies and the spangled blue and green blowflies all talking at once. Every hundred yards or so, it was as if an unseen hand had opened a bucket of butterflies.

This Eden rolled on to the road just up from St Winwaloe's Church in Poundstock. It was the end of the day inside. The pews in the chancel looked as if they were sweetly carved by a long-gone tide, leaving dark fossilised lines now empty of sap: this was a kingdom devoid of butterflies. The graveyard was a good deal more lively, with a gathering of young men and women lying around on the grass all apparently preparing themselves for a wedding.

The road beyond the church rises and falls through the backlands of Cornwall, going nowhere, ending in a choice between two paths. The path on the left runs uphill through a tunnelled hollow way where at times the banks steepen and weave with roots and ferns. Just before where the path ends on the bridleway in Tregole the string net covering of a round straw bale was hanging down from the trees, forming a veil between what went before and what lay beyond. Cornwall exists on a threshold, up until five hundred years ago it stood on the edge of the known world; it embodies the limits of the known and was for generations of Celtic saints and hermits 'a thin place': the natural destination, the starting point for their journeys into the depths of the summer light and what lies beyond the veil of existence.

Tregole, North Cornwall
Start and finish: OS map 111. Grid reference 193980
Time: four hours

▶ I parked in Tregole. From here take the bridleway that heads downhill towards the sea. I could find no trace of the footpath leading over the fields to Trewint. It is marked clearly on the map, so it is there somewhere. I simply headed over the fields, but if you are planning to do that, remember that the stream beds are very deep and not easy to cross.

▶ From Trewint, the footpath was again not obvious at all, but it is there: it runs from Lower Trewint up behind Anthony's house. From Trewint follow an old track down into the Millook Water valley.

▶ Once you reach the stream follow the left-hand bank that runs down to the sea. The path is narrow and steep in places but quite beautiful. After about one-and-a-half miles you will reach the main path to the sea: here it

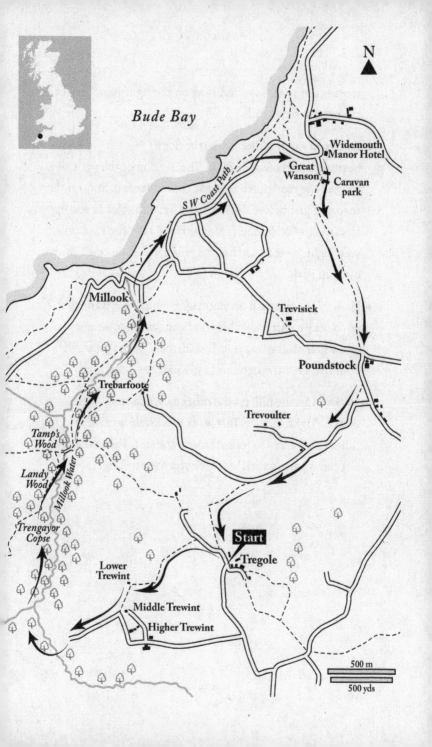

N

Bude Bay

S W Coast Path

Widemouth
Manor Hotel

Great
Wanson

Caravan
park

Millook

Trevisick

Trebarfoote

Poundstock

Trevoulter

Tamp's
Wood

Landy
Wood

Millook Water

Trengayor
Copse

Start

Tregole

Lower
Trewint

Middle Trewint

Higher Trewint

500 m

500 yds

crosses a small bridge and runs on the right-hand side of the stream for a while.

► Once you reach Millook take the South West Coast Path heading north towards Bude. This section of the path follows the road down towards Great Wanson. Stay on the road and just before the left-hand bend that leads you up towards the Widemouth Manor Hotel take the road on your right, next to some Scots pines, until you come to the caravan park.

► Here follow the path on your right, which is just in front of the main entrance. This winds on for about a mile and a half all the way into Poundstock. Once you reach Poundstock, turn right and walk past the church.

► Halfway up the hill, on the other side, is a small path on your right. Take it. This leads to a lovely section of minor road and you follow this to the end. Then take the left-hand path, which will take you back to Tregole.

— WALK 7 —

Guernsey

La Rue qui ne mène nulle part

Forty-four years ago, in a small hotel up the coast from St Peter Port, four children stole a glass from the dining room and placed it on some paper. On the paper was a hastily written alphabet. They summoned the spirits and asked who they would marry and how long they would live. I was to marry someone whose name began with the letter J and was to live until I was eighty-seven. On the last day one of the other children, called Jane, took my hand and looked into my eyes. We were hiding under a bed cover at the time and at that moment I didn't know what to do, so I did nothing. My only other vivid memories that remain from that time are of a mountain of rotting tomatoes left at the edge of a track behind a dark-doored house; the tide lapping against a scallop shell at the bottom of the harbour wall in St Peter Port, and a close-up of some pink shells lying in sunlight and sand on the island of Herm. The other memories are slightly out of focus: my mother sunbathing on the other side of a window in the hotel, some seaweed-covered rocks and a road without a beginning or an end.

The sky was recovering from rain, the clouds beginning to thin and wear into threadbare patches of blue; really I should have walked from the airport. The taxi driver looked exhausted, his eyes only half open, and for three or so miles he flew his crows. Most of the people working in the shops and cafés he said were not from the island. Over the centuries the small population of Guernsey has always been at the mercy of far greater and rapacious forces blowing in from across the sea. The Bretons, Normans, Capetians, the Aragonese, Germans and British have all at some point enforced their will here. And whilst English is spoken, the street names and the vast majority of the house names are French, which somehow makes sense for a sixty-five-square-mile island rising out of the waves between Britain and France. History condenses on islands.

St Peter Port harbour was clogged with yachts, but the backstreets were almost empty except for a few early tourists travelling from window to window. Walking out of town up Fountain Street there was nothing to see behind much of the glass; the businesses had closed, the shelves were bare. The retail quarter peters out at the beginning of La Charroterie, and on the left-hand side of the street are older houses. One three-storey house with greying net curtains that appeared to have atrophied behind green windows had been completely surrounded by men in orange helmets who were standing around in a brown pit that had been dug right the way round the house. Rising on the other side of the road were a series of colourless ten-storey havens that housed the rooms where loopholes, small print and exemptions are stored: the Channel Islands have different tax laws to those of the mainland. As I wandered past, a small coterie of men in suits stood smoking in front of a bland main doorway.

After passing the hospital the road narrows and meanders between houses and the beginnings of fields, most of which are no bigger than two or three tennis courts. It isn't just that the houses and farms have French names, it is something in their shape, their demeanour, their essence; they have a French accent. Maybe it is the sea air, or perhaps the soil, but there didn't seem to be as many roses. The gardens here are the colour of sweets, rhubarb and custard, sherbet lemons, gob-stoppers – a feast of sugared colours. The hedges between the small fields appear to be rounded, they are made of earth and bracken and very few of the fields have crops in them; most are hay meadows that were rich with a second flush of grass. The soil feels compressed, the fecundity sieved and distilled into fine, fertile grains that could unpick the locks on the hardest of husks: there is a sense that should someone stick a broom handle into the earth here, in no time at all it would bud and flower.

There are very few inland paths in Guernsey but the whole island is stitched with little back roads that are light on traffic. Sitting next to the gate of many of the houses on the back roads behind the airport were boxes full of cobwebs. Some of them had rusting cash tins nailed into their base but apart from one which had five yellow and red apples in a Tupperware container, the rest were empty. The dilapidated greenhouse that loomed above a bank of ladies tears was full and packed tight to the roof with imprisoned brambles, an icon of light and warmth turned into a dark and impenetrable house of thorns.

There are not many big trees on the island. A few tall plane trees and a wonderful stand of holm oaks rise next to the road leading out of St Peter Port but in the interior the trees seem younger and smaller. I was on the point of thinking that inland Guernsey had been encased in a terrarium when just as the rue des Buttes feeds into the busier Route de St André I was confronted with a ten-foot-high gorse hedge. I would love to have seen it blazing with yellow flowers and smelling of coconuts.

The little chapel that sits just off the Route de St André is indeed straight out of a terrarium. Built using broken pieces of crockery and shells, it is sixteen feet long and nine feet wide. It is the third incarnation of a chapel built by Brother Déodat, one of the diaspora of many thousands of monks who left France after the French government declared in 1904 that the services of the 'Brothers of Christian Schools' were no longer required. The first little chapel was just nine feet long and four-and-a-half feet wide: it was built in 1914 but deemed too small by the other monks so Brother Déodat demolished it overnight. At nine feet by six feet, the second Chapel was slightly bigger, but not big enough for the Bishop of Portsmouth to get through the door. Firstly I am saddened that in 1923 his attempts to get through the door were not filmed and, I hope that at the time he was wearing a full cope and mitre; and, secondly, I wonder why the Bishop of Portsmouth did not consider that this would have been an ideal time to take on a penance of fasting. Had he done so, the second chapel would surely not have been demolished. On the other side of the doorway leading into the third little chapel is an underwater light. The ceiling is a garden of flowers made out of shells and Mary stands on a tiny altar dressed in her blue-and-white robes, surrounded by untidy candles and scrawled notes of prayers among a thousand broken petals of blue and pink roses.

From the little chapel the road isn't easy; there are some blind corners, but a pavement is about 300 yards further on. It winds all the way to the end of the runway and, from here, onto the Route de Plaisance, where I came across three donkeys in a narrow paddock and behind them a flower garden beaming with dahlias and smelling of marigolds. Next to a gate was a box brimming with tied bunches of flowers. The far end of the garden runs down the side of the Rue des Landes where in a wider paddock two Guernsey cows lay tethered and sleeping. Beyond them in a cropped and feathered enclosure eleven plump white geese slowly sidled towards the gate I was leaning on. There was nothing to indicate the existence of a footpath other than a sign which read 'Riding of motorcycles and horses prohibited. By order of the Constables'. It was more of a track than a path and it led quietly over a small stream then curved on to the Rue de Vidocq.

On the opposite side were a couple of long and tall green-houses; the remains of two cars sat rotting under the glass and the metal arteries of an irrigation system lay in various pieces on the sand-coloured soil, which was littered with flotsam. Sofas, sacks and seed trays, tubing and a scattering of decaying cardboard boxes. A muscular dark-haired man in a grey T-shirt and red shorts stood leaning over a workbench in a smaller glasshouse; he told me the last tomatoes were harvested over twenty years ago and since then the glasshouses had been empty apart from for a short time when they were used for seed germination. Glasshouses cover 7 per cent of the land on Guernsey and the vast majority of them, like the fields, now lie empty.

Five minutes on from the glasshouses, the sea lay brooding and stirring 300 feet below yellow and pink sliding slopes and great fractured slabs of grey cliffs. The outline of the French coast rose in distant brown hills through the damp sea air, and roving across the slate-blue surface of the ocean were white lakes of light with vague edges and no destination. Nothing tethers the sea. The German observation tower looked almost new, as if it had been built last week. What is remarkable is that this corn-coloured stump of concrete is not covered in graffiti. From a distance it resembles the head of an Easter Island statue, but the coral eyes of those statues looked inward over the land; this ghost faces the sea. How long was one watch? Four hours, six hours looking out over the water for boats that never landed, for planes that never appeared?

I remember the first time I watched rain travel over the surface of water. It was in a summer storm and I was fishing on the lake that fills the bottom of the garden at Chartwell in Kent. The light compressed and the wind rallied. The rain hit the far end of the lake first, instantly boiling the water, and in no more than four seconds it swept over the rest of the lake, ruffling the surface into broken pieces of lace. It moved on just as quickly as it had arrived. By then I was drenched to the skin and standing under an oak and as the rush quietened, the water stilled and the sunlight snapped through the branches, setting fire to the leaves. To spend a day simply looking at the sea would change you: even in wartime a year ingesting all that colour and the intimacies of light and movement and you would return home after the war a changed man for reasons very different from those experienced by most combat soldiers.

The Guernsey coast path is more of a combination of driveways and sea roads than a pure path. In this south-east corner, it is not easy walking and there is no single icon; no yellow arrows, or red- and blue-circled markers. Instead, there are stones at ground level with carved inscriptions and arrows pointing towards the next bay or hamlet. At times the path leaves the sea to wander inland under pines, crossing small areas of heathland, taking to a section of road before narrowing and dropping down into coastal valleys, across streams no wider than a book. As I sat down to eat some lunch on a green bench overlooking the sea I thought it could almost have been in North Devon, except there are no fields and no fences, no stiles, and no occasional pepper-coloured shingle beaches. Somewhere between St Peter Port and the green bench the container holding the three-bean salad had split open, covering my waterproof with kidney beans and marinating the very handy spare pair of socks in French dressing. It was hunger that slung the peregrine falcon above me, just an arc of grey slicing downwards then folding its wings into its body to generate the speed needed for an ambush: it is the first peregrine I have seen for a number of years. I love the fact that all I catch of them are glimpses.

The wall butterfly settled for long enough on some rough earth beneath a gorse bush for me to be able to see the blocks of colour built into its wings. Some butterflies are named poetically – the purple emperor, the painted lady, the brimstone. And others, such as the large white, the common blue and the orange-tip, are named descriptively. Most butter-flies were named in the eighteenth and nineteenth centuries. This butterfly was given its name because it appears to favour walls as places to rest while generating the heat needed within its body to fly. When I was a child the wall brown, which is its country name, was common in England, but intensive farming and habitat loss have driven it into the coastal areas; like the speckled wood, it is a dainty butterfly.

On the steeper sections of the coast path the built-in steps are buttressed with concrete. I have not seen steps like them on any other coastal path and they seemed out of place, grumbling a stubborn dissonance to all that thrived around them. Where the valleys flatten out the path enters tunnels through stunted oaks where the dark air is sweetened with the scent of ferns. Just before the land drops down to the small bay of Petit Bôt the path splits; there were no signs, so I chose the steeply descending steps. This was a mistake: they led down to an abandoned gun emplacement platform that is hidden in the cliffs. The alternative was to climb back up again or risk the rocks – there was the smallest of trails leading down from the side of the platform. Where the rocks were dry it was easy enough but the last little section, which drops down into a damp gully, turns slippery and the pools deepen towards the sand. Luckily the tide was out and a thin layer of water seemed stretched over the sand. Petit Bôt is more of a cove with rising cliffs enclosing the small beach which would be gone once the tide came in. Children's voices always blend so beautifully with the sound of the waves.

Sitting outside the beach café were small huddles of silver-haired men and women all wearing pastel-coloured waterproof tops. They were either drinking tea or eating ice creams. The clouds had now swamped the sky and the wind was ruffling hair. I pored over the map. The plan had been to walk back into St Peter Port: I realised it could be done but it would have to be done in a hurry.

There are probably four main walking speeds. The slowest is ambling. Cows making their way to be milked amble; and people in love tend to walk together at ambling speed. When I am looking for cep and chanterelle mushrooms, it is an amble. Then there's strolling. A one-mile stroll takes twice as long as a one-mile walk, but it also takes in twice as much. On Friday and Saturday evenings in the cities and towns of Italy the *passegiata* marks a break between the end of the working day and the enjoyment of the evening, people still promenade. They dress up and take to wandering up and down certain streets; they do this to see others and to be seen. Promenading is walked at a strolling speed. When Astrud Gilberto sings 'Tall and tan and young and lovely the girl from Ipanema goes walking', 'the girl' was promenading, she was strolling.

Walking is the fastest and most naturally comfortable speed to travel; just slow enough for detail still to penetrate through the rhythm and fast enough for you to be able to cover twenty-five miles a day. Hurrying is walking as fast as your legs will take you; all details are lost at hurrying speed, the land blurs, and in a hurry I have trodden on butterflies, not seen ice or noticed the incoming rain. In the West the dial has reached hurrying speed – we hurry from home to the airport, from screen to screen not noticing what is being trampled, we were never there.

I loved the stroll up the Route du Petit Bôt, the small stream sliding down the side of the road feeding long lines of ladies tears. Great thick fuchsia bushes ringing with two-tone pinks, purples and reds. And in just about every garden robust and big-leaved temperate palms. Halfway up the hill the road bends past the Manor Hotel, which housed visiting German officers during the war. It feels out of the way, alone in a dungeon of trees, as if there is still an unfound Luger under the floorboards. After about half a mile the road winds into Forest, passing a bus stop which, when I saw it, was submerged in hanging baskets; it had become almost a shrine of flowers singing to the concrete around it. I ventured into the local store in search of something to eat and asked the woman on the till whether the store sold any local tomatoes. She pointed me towards a cardboard box lying on the floor just outside the door. Apart from these few tomatoes and the local paper, everything else was imported.

There is something forlorn here, like a blind daffodil, a dog lost in a city. When, later on, I called the Guernsey Ministry of Agriculture a man confirmed that currently it is not economically viable to grow food crops on the island. A handful of specialist growers remain, some growing herbs and others organic vegetables. But the plain fact is that in Guernsey you are walking through an empty larder, there is nothing to eat here other than money. None of the previous invading forces blown in from across the sea laid waste to the land as successfully as the forces of economics are doing right now.

Just before the airport I followed a small lane down towards the church of St Marguerite de la Forêt. Beyond the church is a wild tuft of land no bigger than a pond, painted onto an old piece of wood strung round a tree were the words 'The vicarage wild garden'. It wasn't used; there looked to be the remains of a path which ran around a small sunken area in the middle, but it felt undisturbed. I stepped into the shade and stood for a while watching the ever present wind move the light on the underside of the leaves, turning them into jewels. This is intimacy. How many thousand shrines did I miss today?

Guernsey.

Start/finish: States of Guernsey official map.

Grid reference 384449

Time: four hours

▶ From the town church in Saint Peter Port walk up Fountain street and then onto Le Bordage.

▶ At the top of Le Bordage, turn left and follow La Charroterie upwards. This road effectively feeds into Ruettes Brayes, which you should follow right up to the T junction at the top of the town. Here cross the road and follow La Rue de la Corbinerie past the hospital.

▶ After about half a mile, take a left-hand turn into Rue des Huriaux and cross over a minor road. After about five hundred yards the road bends sharply round to your left: keep going as it merges with Rue des Landes. After a quarter of a mile or so this then merges with Rue des Naftiaux and comes to a crossroads.

▶ Here, cross over and follow Rue des Hougues, which in time joins Rue des Buttes. This runs all the way to the main road where you turn left.

▶ Route de Saint André is 400 yards on your left: take it. This leads past the little chapel and merges into Route de l'Issue, which ends at a T junction.

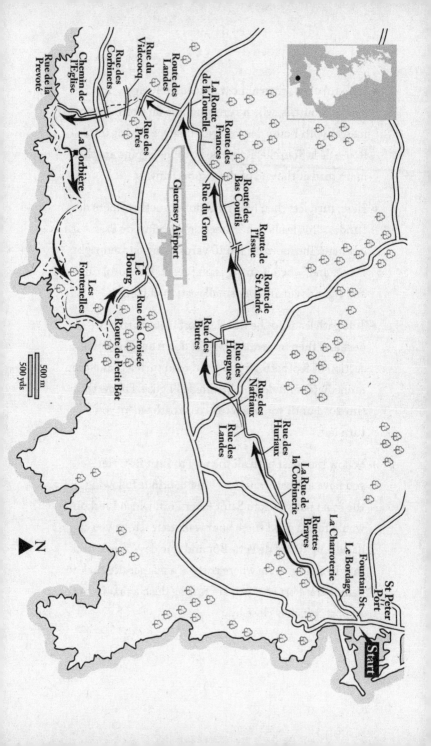

▶ Here turn left, then almost immediately right, into Rue des bas Courtils, which runs into Rue du Gron. This road merges with Route des Frances, finally evolving into Route de la Tourelle. Route de la Tourelle joins another main road at the end of the airport runway.

▶ Here, turn left then first right down another Route des Landes. This leads to a T junction with Rue de Prés: turn left here. The footpath is 110 yards along on your right: take it and, when it emerges on Rue du Videcocq, turn left and right down another small section of path.

▶ This path leads to the Rue des Corbinets: turn left here and then immediately right down another small section of footpath. At the main road turn left and then immediate right down Chemin de l'Eglise. Follow this tiny road until you reach the coast path where you turn left.

▶ Follow the coast path all the way to Petit Bôt. Here you have a choice: you can either continue following the coast path back to Saint Peter Port, which I reckon would take a good three hour walk to reach, or you can dawdle up Route de Petit Bôt and Rue des Croisée back into Le Bourg, from where there is a bus service back to Saint Peter Port or if you are feeling flush a taxi from the airport, which is close by.

Wanton Walls, the Scottish borders

Venus in firs

Just to the east of the town of Lauder the land bubbles into smooth, round hills with deep valleys set between them. There is an emptiness here: it is not that there are no houses – it is just that the spaces between them are greater, the fields seem squarer and the hedges are straighter. Set into the land are deep green stands of conifer plantations. And without them the emptiness would be amplified. This has always been a hinterland, a space between, the home of the reivers, rustlers; of shifting allegiances and fragile alliances. The Romans did not colonise this land.

Wanton Walls is one farm and about six houses, all of which seemed to be empty. I knocked on each door, wanting to ask if I could leave the car on a tarmacked area that sloped down in front of the concrete foundations of an unbuilt house, but no one answered. A council lorry turned up with three men sitting in the front seat. I am not sure whether I couldn't decipher a word the driver said because he had a mouth full of sandwich or because his accent was too much for my southern brain. I didn't fare much better with the farmer on the quad bike but we kind of managed in the end with sign language and I got the gist: the men in the council lorry were just about to re-tar the road so I should move the car back a bit.

The main farmhouse rests on a small plateau halfway up a hill with long views south down towards the border, which must be no more than thirty miles away. Washing had been hung over a clothes horse to dry in the small conservatory, which perched above a newly mown lawn. Swallows were gathering on the phone lines between the house and a hamlet of barns that housed hills of sand-coloured grain and neatly parked tractors, there wasn't a breath of wind.

The Southern Upland Way runs down through the middle of the farm and continues heading upwards, passing a cream-painted coloured concrete house that belongs to Scottish Water. It was empty, with grass growing in the cracks of the driveway; ghosts sleep in empty houses. Once past this house the track ran between two bright fields of uncut barley – when barley is ripe, the seed heads hang down towards the earth, as if the whole field is in prayer.

It was early September and, looking out south across the land, I could see many fields still to be harvested. A huge wall of conifers stood where the barley gave out: this is the edge of Edgarhope Wood and it was as silent on the inside as it is on the map. There was not even the lightest of breezes, the pine trees were stock still. Nothing stirred, not a foot or a wing; it was as if every mouse had been rounded up and every bird had been sold. I looked for deer signs on the banks that rose along the edge of the track but there wasn't a hoof print to be found: nothing ruffled the needle-carpeted floor leading into the dark cellars of the wood. Conifer plantations exist without any hint of mercy, the trees are packed in as tightly as battery hens. In time every blade of grass, every bramble, everything on the ground that lives on sunlight dies.

Wandering further into the wood, it was as if I were entering a land that had recently been attacked. Whole trees lay on the side of the path. They hadn't been cut – they had been pulled out by their roots; they were not arranged or stacked, they were left where they were dropped, like rubbish. Some had broken trunks, others were torn, but most of them simply lay there rusting. A couple of hundred yards further on the entire right-hand side of the track was a no man's land of twisted brush. A handful of dead trees stood amidst this carnage but the rest had gone. It was as if the land had been burgled and in the process of stealing the trees the thieves had covered their tracks by leaving nothing unbroken. Maybe this is the best way – having harvested the trees, to call insects, birds and mammals back into this space – but it didn't feel that way. Growing out of the rubble was the next generation of pines planted as close together as the previous one, primed to foster another world as dark and desolate as the hearts that created this one.

Perhaps this path wasn't meant to be walked. The only sign of life I saw was a lone red admiral butterfly patrolling the edges of the track, dancing over the ruins, unencumbered by the fascination of carnage. After about three-quarters of a mile I reached another wall of trees and wandered back into the permanent shade. Where the path turns sharply the gap between the wood and the fields to the north is at its narrowest. It looked as if this way is regularly walked, as the fence had been trodden down. Here the remains of an old track stretch upwards and the space between sections of the plantation is wide enough for a green carpet of grass and a couple of mature oaks. There are feathers on the ground, it is an alleyway of life – what is immediately noticeable is the presence of birds. The track comes to an end where it meets the field on the other side of an old gate that marks the boundary between the plantation and the open land.

I was looking for a track that peters out near to where the gate stands. A track is a farming route; most farms generally have one main track running through them. Many of these farm tracks are hedged on both sides and in high summer they are rivers of colour and life as the verges swell and the space between the tyre ruts fills up with flowers. They are working routes used to move cows and sheep from one field to another or to ferry trailers full of grain from the fields to the barns; they are not plumbed into the network of paths and for most of the year they are secluded and empty of footsteps.

Bridleways vary in width, some are little wider than footpaths and others are considerably wider than farm tracks; these were once the main routes between towns and villages. I love the bridleways that run over heathlands and the high moors, great wide swathes of pockmarked sandy earth winding their way above the rest of the world and I love how a slow autumn evening when the distance is turning a dirty mauve makes its way into my bed.

A 'Way' is a longer path such as the South Downs Way and the Pennine Way. Many of these were old pilgrim routes although newer ones have been created by joining sections of bridleways and footpaths together. There are now over 300 waymarked paths in Britain, many of them running for over a hundred miles; to my knowledge, no one has walked all of them.

A footpath is in most cases just about wide enough for two people to walk arm in arm, but many of the delightful paths that cross the fields connecting villages are now very much single file. Strangely, the footpaths that pass through woodlands tend to be slightly wider.

I am not sure I found the track running up the east side of the plantation, as the grass in the field was up to my knees. There were places where it might have been, but they may well have been just the lie of the land. The footpath was plain enough, emerging on the other side of some sturdy hawthorns, a bed of stubborn grey stones lit by the sun and as dry as the grass on either side of it. Lighting up within the grass were patches of pink heather, hints of what was to come.

As I rounded the corner under Dabshead Hill the fields gave way to a pink expanse of moorland. The gate divided two worlds: one world existed on one side of the gate and a different world existed on the other, it was that immediate. Three grouse broke cover and flew out low over the land and I could hear others gargling nearby. A few hard-looking sheep trotted off and the air began to smell of honey. Every so often there would be flashes of silver bouncing off the surface of black water pools that were otherwise invisible; and out to the east as far as the eye could see there wasn't a tree or a house or a telegraph pole: there was nothing but rolling pink land.

Looking into the distance can stop time. I'm not sure how long I stood there, surveying the land. To the north-east the deep valley of Earnscleuch Water cuts down between the hills, and growing next to the burn were occasional trees in various early shades of autumn. It is not a long track that leads over the moor and in time it reaches a gate that leads back into grasslands. Here the path simply disappears, so I made for what looked like the stone circle on the map.

The trouble was, in each field there are piles of stones and distinguishing between what is a cairn and what is simply a heap of fieldstones was almost impossible. So using the dead trees left at the top of the plantation as a marker, I cut through several big fields and found a rough stone path that breaks on to the Southern Upland Way. The stone walls here are tall and thick, great straight grey lines running through the landscape. Many of the metal gates in the walls are bent and battered; metal gates tend to be cheaper than wooden ones and by rights should last longer, but most of these looked as if they had been run over.

The cattle must have seen the top of my head bobbing along on the other side of wall. I heard them coming towards me, a thunder in the ground growing louder until they reached the other side of the wall; then I could hear them hustling and breathing loudly as their heavy scent leached into the air. They followed me all the way down to the bottom of a valley, where a group of them had broken clean through a fence into an area of newly planted trees. Something must have spooked them as they made a dash for it, running clean through another section of fence and out into the field to join the rest of the herd.

There were two choices: the first was to follow the path through another field of mothers with calves, or take my chances in the new plantation, which the other cattle had just vacated, and head through the trees to an empty field on the other side. As I walked through the plantation, the posse of young bullocks that had just run out of the trees charged back towards the fence they had just run through. I made a dash for the end of the wood and clattered over a broken stile just as they pulled up inches short of the wire. The reason why the gates are so battered and the walls are so thick became blindingly clear.

On the other side of the stile a small burn crept through a deep channel sunk in a wild weave of grass and sedge. In a steeply rising field next to the mothers and calves one mushroom lay flat in the grass. Looking back to the other side of the valley, I spotted a squat little corrugated iron barn with peeling paint the colour of haws sitting alone in some heather. It looked vaguely Indian. Then the rising tones of a quad bike came from the field of mothers and calves and I watched as the driver came over the hill. I saw him notice me and turn the handles towards me. He drew the bike to a halt on the other side of the fence, and turned off the engine. 'Hi there,' he said. He had a full head of grey hair and was wearing a countryman's shirt. 'Did you decide not to walk through the cows and their calves?' he asked. 'Yes, I did,' I replied. He was silent for a moment then replied, 'That was the wise choice.' There was nothing unfriendly about him. I asked him about the barn and he said that in the past it had only been used in winter to store the hay with which to feed the sheep when the wind comes looking for bones in January and February, but it wasn't used anymore as the sheep were now wintered back at the farm.

We talked about the Scottish referendum and about lambing; we stood for a good ten minutes and then he offered me directions up to the edge of the plantation. I followed a wall down to where the path meets the plantation and runs through the far section of the wood before reaching the edge of the fields and sloping back down between the barley. Coming up from the farm was a young mother; she had a young girl in the saddle of the horse she was leading and another holding her other hand. We all said hello. At the farm the sun was out on the empty yards and in one of the barns something metal was being mended. The three men in the lorry hadn't sprayed the road.

It is only now, as this walk comes to an end as I sit here in the quiet of night, that I am beginning to know and be grateful; to be thankful that I live in a land of paths where two strangers can meet in the middle of nowhere and have a conversation.

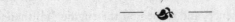

Wanton Walls, the Scottish Borders

Start and finish: Landranger Map 73.
Grid reference 483548
Time: three-and-a-half hours

....

▶ There is a good place to park next to the concrete
  foundations of a house that sits just in front of the other
  six or so houses in Wanton Walls. But I would ask the
  farmer for permission, just to make sure.

▶ Walk up through the farm, following the Southern
  Upland Way. Once you reach Edgarhope Wood turn left
  and follow the track for about a mile and a half. After
  going through what is an area that has been newly
  planted, the path winds downhill through the conifer
  plantation and arrives at a left-hand corner.

▶ There is an old track that leads up between two sections
  of conifer plantation: it runs uphill for about 300 yards
  and then you will come to a gate and open land.

▶ Once over the gate, head up to your left until you reach
  the path running round Dabshead Hill. This leads round
  and out over a gate on to Edgarhope Moor.

▶ Follow the path until it comes to a gate and some fields.
  Here the path is very hard to find, so it is best to head in
  a north-easterly direction over the fields until you reach

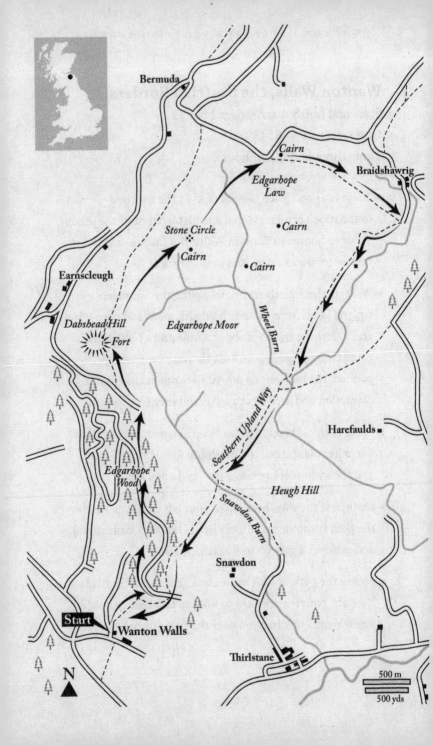

the Southern Upland Way, which is waymarked with yellow markers.

▶ At the Southern Upland Way turn right and follow this path all the way back to Wanton Walls.

Bures, Suffolk

One white horse

What becomes apparent while driving through various villages in East Anglia is that there are definitely more people with blond hair in this part of the world: this genetic trait harks back to the time when this section of England was Danish. The map of England drawn in the year 884 not only shows the extent of the territory held by the Danes, but also describes just under half of East Anglia as 'swampland'.

It is lovely arriving after dark simply because your surroundings remain a mystery until the morning. I woke up in a warm house in an Edwardian backstreet in Sudbury, and then set off for the village of Bures, which is pronounced with a *pure* in it. These late September mornings can be so tender, especially when everything is still; the temporal turns eternal and, having made seeds and fruits, the earth, it seems, is resting. The village of Bures sits on the River Stour hugged into the slightly rolling land on a line on the map where Suffolk meets Essex. Whilst it was very much part of Danish Britain, it wasn't however part of the swamp that now exists as the defiant and fabulous Fenlands, which lie to the north of here. Bures is neat; not quite a postcard, it is a steady village on a river where I would imagine the owner of the post office can order the newspapers in the afternoon knowing exactly who is going to buy each one of them the next morning.

From the west side of the bridge the path heads north. I wish it had followed the river but it cut straight along the side of a field that had already been ploughed and drilled with next year's crop. It must have been just a matter of days between the harvest and the sowing. There is nothing that is nurturing about this practice: just like us, the soil is a living organism and it needs rest. After about half a mile the path does briefly reach the river, where it emerges into a small field of pasture with a very handsome weeping willow in the middle of it along with a relaxed little coterie of cows and calves. On the river, which seemed almost solid, was a pair of mute swans. I have never seen a swan in a hurry. Swans live slowly, unless their young are threatened, at which point they don't defend – they attack. Mute swans usually mate for life, which is why single swans have an air of loneliness around them: it can be very lonely being individually beautiful. In heraldry, mute swans represent a love of music and poetry, all unmarked mute swans in this country belong to the Queen. There is a legend that mute swans sing sweetly before they die, which is the origin of the phrase 'swan song'.

They were the only wild birds I had seen since leaving

Bures and there were none in Lamarsh, which lies just beyond the river. There is a pub and some big separate houses with clean cars on swept driveways, a little row of bungalows but not a feather on any of the lawns; the only sign of life was a solitary comma butterfly dancing its own swan song over a patch of nettles which were holding out against a wasteland. In the porch of the church, which sits neatly on the edge of the village, are passport-sized photographs of faces under which are written their job titles – 'Rural Dean, Archdeacon, youth worker, treasurer' – and for a dreadful moment I believed they might speak of heaven. Here sadly stands another country church that is locked.

From the brow of a hill beyond the church the course of the river within the land became clearer. It was marked by evenly spaced trees planted along its banks: this is the doing of the dead eyes of order – and had the untidy rushes been cleared away? the ripples monitored, the flies counted? I was rescued from this tight hand by a white horse galloping round a field for what appeared to be no reason other than that he wanted to, snorting and kicking up his back legs as he ran, dislodging great clods of earth and jettisoning them into the air behind. A galloping horse echoes a beating heart. I picked a handful of a grass and hung it over the fence, 'horse clicking' the back of my mouth. The galloping stopped, the heartbeat slowed and this beautiful animal simply stood still looking at me from the middle of the field for a while before trotting over. He was still breathing heavily heaving in air when he reached my hand before gently taking the grass from my palm. A few tears began to appear in the cloud but the sun was struggling to melt away the rain that had fallen in the night; the air was warmer but the grass was still cold: I was now in Essex.

Walking down the hill towards Valley Farm is to move through a complete change of ethos: the hedges hadn't been beaten and there were great tits, blackbirds and a wood pigeon somewhere singing, their song a lesson in how to relax. Beyond Valley Farm is a wild field with a stream flowing through the middle of it and huddled into the corner was a caravan, a lair in which to read and hole up with a torch, and, when the autumn winds arrive, to fall asleep with the sound of rain on metal.

On both sides of the stream the grass was crawling with crane flies, daddy-long-legs, who always seem to be involved in a perpetual struggle against gravity, as if flying, for them, is only the result of a supreme individual effort; they seem to pedal through the air. I had spoken to a friend a couple of days ago who had dashed out of her house leaving all the lights on and, she also left the front door open. When she returned, the house had been completely overrun with daddy-long-legs – she said there must have been well over a thousand that had slunk in through the open door. They only live for between ten and fifteen days and seem to die drunk on the floor, or they end up as rags in cobwebs.

Crane flies appear to be at their most abundant in what is a strange three-week period running over the last ten days in September and the first ten days of October when it is neither autumn nor summer: a kind of space between the two where nothing happens or feels certain, when there is no movement.

After I'd waded through an uncomfortable field of sugar beet, I found the path reached a minor road, which crosses the stream again just before Loshhouse Farm, which is now a nature reserve run by the Essex Wildlife Trust. Coming down the road on a bicycle was an elderly gentleman dressed in very bright tight Lycra. He was the only person I had seen since setting off and he stopped to ask if he was heading in the right direction for Great Henny. We looked at the map and he started sighing. 'I don't like this road, there are too many bends,' he said. 'It's a country lane,' I replied. 'This is how they are unless you head for the Fens.' He shook his head and pedalled off for what was clearly going to be a very annoying morning.

The geese at Sparrow's Farm, a little further up the road, were a good deal more than annoyed to see me: they raised their necks and started shouting. There was no choice but to walk through them as the path was nowhere to be found. They hissed and spat and a couple of them lowered their necks to the ground and spread their wings. I know this posture well: it is the last thing they do before they charge. Male geese, or ganders, are born with courage in their blood. They are incredibly protective of female geese, which have the delightful soubriquet of 'dames'. The stand-off lasted for about a minute, after which they slowly sauntered off jeering, with their heads held high. There was no need on this occasion for either of us to get entangled in a flurry of feathers and expletives. Brokering peace terms with a goose is always more pleasurable than dealing with a dog in the same mood. Geese don't have teeth.

Beyond the geese, the path runs up through a little copse of oaks and bracken, and then over a field under some pylons into the village of Twinstead. This was the second footpath that had again been ploughed up so I asked a woman who was tending to a hedge who owned the land. She explained it was owned by a man in the village but he no longer farmed it. This meant one of two things: that it was either rented out to a local farmer or it was 'contract farmed'. The rosy view of a family looking after a farm, and the way of life that goes with it, isn't becoming more and more sepia – there are many thriving family farms – but in the south-east especially there is a new dynamic driving the practicalities of who farms the land. Some of the eye-watering and dysfunctional bonuses and salaries being paid in the City of London are ending up in six-bedroom farmhouses. Thirty years ago a farmer who was coming to the end of his days with a 200-acre farm, and who had no family members to take it on, would probably have sold it along with the farmhouse. The local farmers farming the land traditionally would have come in and bought twenty or thirty acres, and by doing so all of them would have slightly increased the size of their own landholding; this way of doing things has been happening quietly for generations. With house and land prices as they are now, very few of us can afford a six-bedroom farmhouse along with 180 acres of Essex. Another factor is that death duties are not payable on landholdings, so for those with a lot of money in their pockets land is somewhere safe to put it.

Once the house and the land are bought, the land is rented out either to a neighbouring farmer or to a contract farmer. Contract farmers tend to farm many different pieces of land, sometimes many miles apart, which means effectively that the link between the land and those who live within it is broken. The relationship between human beings and the land is both practical and sentimental; and at best perhaps romantic. A hedge becomes more than just a hedge when I know that my grandfather planted it, a path becomes part of me when I know my mother walked it, and it is this emotional continuity that is the unseen currency of the countryside: that this might be my father's land, but it is also very much the land of my fathers and my mothers, and I can know them through it and in it; and what is passed down is not only a visceral intimacy but also a legacy of care.

If it hadn't been for the woman tending her hedge on the edge of the village I would have assumed that all the houses in Twinstead were empty. After just a hundred yards or so on the road the path leads through a narrow passageway running alongside the backs of garages and a small sunken pond surrounded by flagstones glimpsed through a thicket of bamboo. Turning a corner, you come to a neatly cut waist-high hedge, on the other side of which there is a mown lawn with an arbour placed in the middle of it; beyond that a kaleidoscopic feast of pinks, purples, scarlet, oranges, mauves and yellows, a border full of azaleas in bloom. Not only had the owners cut the hedge on the side of the path, which was extremely generous of them, but because it was so low it was as if I had walked into their garden. Walking from wild or farmed land directly into a garden, especially a flower garden, is always a vivid experience. A flower garden is a held space: we create a garden like this mostly for nothing other than pleasure, the pleasure it gives. Very rarely does wild nature house such an intense mix of closely packed primary colours; a coral reef may be the only exception. I do not share Dorothy Gurney's conviction that 'One is nearer God's Heart in a garden.' What one is surely nearer to is the reality of intimacy, an intimacy between human beings and the earth, petals, roots and seeds. In the belief that this relationship mirrors the intimate nature of divine love, gardens are associated with Paradise in many religions. In the Christian tradition Easter Sunday morning begins with Christ standing alone in a garden. Coming straight off the empty fields and into a flower garden with an arbour on a bright green lawn heightens the sense of how truly other-worldly gardens can be.

Reality, if there is such a thing in the singular sense, was round the next corner, where some steps led over a wall past a rather beautifully dilapidated Victorian stable block and then out onto another mute and empty field. I heard the machine before I saw it. Entering the side of a wood the sound grew louder and there, through the tips of the leaves I could see it now, a large tractor with what appeared to be an A-frame attached to the back: jangling and clanking, straight out of an underworld, it appeared to be waiting. As I approached, it roared and jerked then careered off down the field hissing out plumes of white poison. I waited in the little wood for a while to let these toxins settle – breathing them is not a good idea; swallowing them is an even worse one. On the other side of the field the path drops down into valley then up slightly, running alongside a much larger wood before crossing a field to a minor road where horseshoe prints had set into the tarmac, a reminder of a much hotter day. The sun strained its way through a layer of high thin cloud, giving an even light that warmed the air, but it wasn't strong enough to lay down any shadows.

At this time of year all the leaves have lost their shine. They are still green but they are brittle and are dying of thirst and the blackberries have turned meagre and mean, but the brambles are sweet and heady. I used to assume they were all blackberries but they are not. Blackberries have thicker stems and bigger thorns, and the fruit begins to ripen towards the end of July. By mid-September they are pretty much done and it is the bramble with its much more compact fruit and superior flavour that hangs down in little bunches from the hedges and all too often, just like the best of fruits are tantalisingly just out of reach. In English folklore the devil is supposed to piss on all the brambles on Old Michaelmas Eve, which is on the night of 10 October, and, yes, beyond that date they do begin to fester and rot, but there can still be a few shiny ones left in early November.

About a mile further on is Whitelands Fruit Farm, a large open drive and a garden shed of a farm shop. The door was open and inside it smelt of summer but there was only one small tray of apples, some jewellery that looked as if it had been made and packed by children and – most out of place – a delightful brown and orange framed tapestry of a barn, hanging on the wooden wall. I don't know why but a creeping sense of guilt started to murmur in me as I stood alone in the shop, maybe because I hadn't been welcomed in. I felt I had slipped in like a thief, unnoticed. Stepping outside I called but no one appeared, the place was completely quiet. Walking back out along the road, I found some plums were hanging on to a branch which had strayed over the hedge; they were perfect in every way and I did feel like a thief after that.

Beyond the fruit farm is a black-earthed path that was musty and muddy: it must have been the soil, there is nothing really thriving here – even the nettles are pale and thin; this is the land of rats. It is not that nothing can thrive where they live, it is that they choose to live in the places where nothing thrives and they should have our admiration for that. The air warmed distinctly at the end of the path and as I headed back towards Bures the last thing I expected to see were two hornets grappling on the road opposite Peyton Hall Farm. I had only ever seen one before in England. Gingerly, I took a closer look. They are twice the size of wasps; longer and larger, hornets appear to be made of razor blades and chlorine. These ones were fighting over who should have the last morsels of summer.

The path back to Bures begins as a wide drove through a wood, but it slowly narrows and sinks, becoming at times just a thread through the nettles. I saw one wren, who landed on a hazel branch and berated me for about five seconds before flying off and becoming a blur. She was shouting a question and the question was: where have I taken her brothers and sisters, her mothers and fathers? The emotional continuity inherent in the land is mapped in more than just hedges, fields and paths and it is earthed in much more than just the human stories it tells. It holds the stories of each leaf, each wing, every song and petal, feather, blade and scale. Speaking to elderly countrymen and women, they will tell of a childhood illuminated by huge flocks of lapwings and skies stippled with starlings, clouds of gatekeepers and meadow brown butterflies, adders under woodpiles and glow-worms lighting up the edges of woods on dreamy July evenings. What they are telling us is that the natural world was much more vivid then than it is now, that it is the diversity of abundance that is the joy of the land.

Bures, Suffolk

Start and finish: OS map 196. Grid reference 904340
Time: four hours

▸ The path begins on the west side of the bridge and heads north. Carry on past the river across the railway line and up to where the path joins a minor road: here turn right.

▸ About a hundred yards after the church there is Stour Valley Path on your left. Take it. This leads to the brow of a hill and continues, bearing right along the edge of some fields. The path ends on a minor road, and here you turn left.

▸ Half a mile further on is a path on your right, just set back within a parking area. Take this path, which heads downhill past Valley Farm and then over the stream.

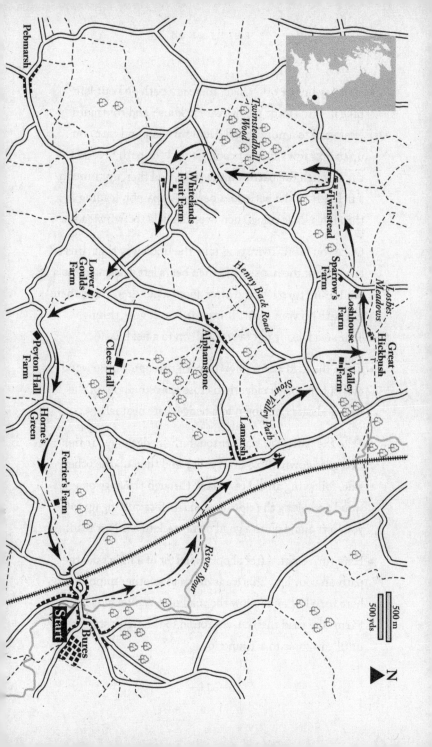

▶ Halfway up the other side, there is a path on your left: take it – this leads past Great Hickbush and continues westward to a minor road. Here turn left and carry on up to Sparrow's Farm. I couldn't find the path here so I cut through the barns on the right, and then up through a field where the path does become apparent, leading through a little copse then over the field to Twinstead.

▶ Once you reach Twinstead take the bridleway that runs at the back of the houses and then bears left, leading on to a road. Here turn left and after about a hundred yards there is a path on your right. This path, which goes through Twinstead, leads out over a wall on to a field.

▶ Cross the field and follow the path through a little wood and out the other side; then cross the remainder of the field and carry on down to a hedge; here bear left.

▶ Take the path that leads through the hedge on your right; this goes down into a little valley and then up the other side, following an old cart track through the edge of a wood and along the side of a field, before cutting up to your left along quite a good farm track to a minor road.

▶ Here turn right. After about a quarter of a mile take the path on your left. This leads down to another minor road: here turn left and follow the road past Whitelands Fruit Farm. The road then curves round to the right; stay on it until you come to a T-junction.

▶ Here turn right and take the path immediately on your left and follow it past a very dark pond to Lower Goulds Farm: here turn right and take the dark-earthed path, which leads to another minor road.

▶ When you reach it turn left, walking past Peyton Hall Farm. Follow the road to another T-junction and turn left again. The path leading back into Bures is on the right, about 600 yards along.

Bedham, West Sussex

Windows in the trees

The boundary where a woodland begins and ends is liminal space. You step literally from the world of fields and sky into a place of shadows and echoes, everything changes: the colours of feathers, the sizes of eyes, the lengths of leaves, the scent of rain. Six thousand years ago this island was wooded; it was the Agricultural Revolution that cleared it of trees, eventually giving us boundaries and roads, chainsaws and gleaming cities. But all this has its antecedent in bronze axes and men and boys wrestling stumps out of the ground to create a field: all fields were created.

Woods have traditionally been cast as the keepers of our shadows or as places of sanctuary from the despots of the cleared land. Stepping into a wood from a field is always vivid as our voices naturally become quieter because we know we may not necessarily see someone who is seeing us; we tend to look behind us more often. It is a natural response. Once I enter the wood it changes me: I become more alert, my hearing more concentrated, I am less inclined to daydream, I am slightly nearer to the reality of my own death and much more present because of it.

It had just finished raining when I arrived in the Mens, a woodland in West Sussex, just beyond Billingshurst. The early autumn leaves on the trees were heavy with water, the air was still and smelt of beer and everything was dripping. When the sun came out the wood lit up into a fairground, glittering and swaying. I am underwater in a sunlit wood. There is actually more woodland now than there was at the beginning of the twentieth century, when wooded areas accounted for no more than 5 per cent of the land area of these lovely islands. That figure has now recovered to 11 per cent, but much of this woodland consists of commercial conifer forests. These become dark, lifeless realms where not even the corpses of pigeons and rabbits are eaten.

There is something uniquely generous about planting a deciduous wood. Those who do so may have to endure stands of saplings which often have a barren air about them, like the feeling created by rows of empty new-built houses; those who plant deciduous woods can do so only because they have imagination, they have seen the cathedrals they are to become; all of these woods are gifts from people long gone, whom we have never met.

This walk began on a wet minor road that tunnelled through trees before swinging round through the tight little hamlet of Hawkhurst Court, which has an air of cups and saucers about it. I saw nothing that belonged to a child, not a swing or a bright pink bicycle. There are now some villages in Cornwall and Devon that have no children living in them at all and there is a lot of talk of the village shop closing, and then the pub, and finally the church. But it is actually when villages no longer have children living in them that something about them dies; they harden and turn in on themselves, the feeling is palpable. Children skip, they undo beautifully all the imposed adult order, they summon the Gods of mischief and delight, they sing – and when they are set free in a place they really loosen it up.

Just beyond Hawkhurst Court the path sinks down into the woods where, thankfully, some laughter was seeping through the trees. As the path unwound I found a small group of men, each with a large rake or two balanced on their shoulders, standing around indulging in a little pre-work chat: they really were going to mow a meadow and, being retired, they knew the song. I remember singing it as a child, bouncing along on the back seats of cars: 'One man went to mow, went to mow a meadow, one man and his dog Spot, bottle of pop, old man Rider had a cow went to mow a meadow.'

Fields and meadows are hundreds of years old, most of them older than the trees that sometimes surround them. In each one of those years the meadow would have been mown. Progress has done away with the mowing, it is not needed any more. First the meadow was mown, and the grass was left as it was to dry. It was then raked into piles and, finally, stooks. Hay meadows are no longer mown in the old sense: instead the hay is cut and bailed. This usually happens in June or July when there are a few hot days to come; and while the cut grasses are drying in the sun, they drop their seeds, which in turn become next year's meadow. The reason why these men were going to mow a meadow was because it was situated in the middle of the wood so it was not possible to get a tractor in there.

I wished I had asked what the meadow was called. It is the names of meadows and fields that have arrived and settled, losing over time the source of how the names came into being that are so mysterious and evocative. The Great Sparks, the Guzzle, Little Turk's Eye, Common Hungerlands – these are just a few of the names of meadows and fields around my home village. But more than that the meadow is, for the English at least, the emblem of how we see ourselves in relation to the land, the root of our belonging; it is part of how we understand who we are. For the Germans and Scandinavians it is the forest, the Greeks have the olive grove; for the peoples of the Middle East it is the garden. The Americans have the road and the Scots the glen. These archetypal gardens are places of beginning, of courtship, of resolution, and when we have endured our struggles, our triumphs, defeats and tears, it is to the meadow we return. The boy leads the man home, to appreciate and to accept the call of intimacy and to know his life is made and measured in the quiet unfolding of days.

I left the meadow men to grapple with an enormous lawnmower they were hauling out of the back of a van, then continued along what is one of the most beautiful woodland paths I have ever trodden. It was from the pages of a fairy tale. I was walking a straight line through a circular space which, as it led gently uphill, became a holloway. A holloway is an ancient path that over time and thousands upon thousands of footsteps and wheels is worn down beneath the level of the land around it. Some holloways have become utterly separated from the land around them, they are too narrow for tractors to use and too deep to fill in. As a result many of their entrances are overgrown and they have to be found: they have become secrets. This holloway emerged on to a small metalled road and led into the hamlet of Bedham. There isn't a big house in Bedham; there are cottages wrapped up in trees, each of them very different from the others and none of them facing in the same direction.

My own directions had become a little hazy and I was peering at the map when a very large maroon four-by-four pulled up. 'Are you lost?' the driver asked. 'Not quite,' I replied. The gentleman who asked me the question then got out of the car and proceeded to show me exactly where I was and how to find the path back to where I needed to be. He also explained that further up the path was an abandoned church that was built, he said, in the 1880s by the Member of Parliament for Midhurst, who was concerned that the people of Bedham were becoming increasingly feral; and that up until the end of the First World War Bedham had been a community of woodsmen. In a land where the meadow means so much, those living in the middle of woods and forests have always been looked upon as outsiders to a certain degree and have been tainted unfairly primarily as the carriers of our own shadows.

I have never seen an isolated church in the middle of a wood before. It was a church built in the shadows, sunk under the trees, it had the feel of a wreck lying in silence on the ocean floor. It was built simply from bricks, and the walls are rounded, not angular, there is no glass in any of the windows and the roof is gone, fallen and stolen. But there is an overriding sense of comfort here and it has that rare resonance of a place of prayer. It was built as both a school and a church and still is the church of St Michael and All Angels. By all accounts angels don't use doors, they just appear and disappear. I have never seen an angel but I once felt an angel's presence. I knew immediately it was an angel and that that was for me to discern; nothing was said, not in words. It was the first night in a new house where we had arrived before I started training to become a priest. At about four in the morning I was woken by a presence in the bedroom that was clear, comforting and beautiful. Churches are boxes – we keep angels in them, we keep eternity in them – but rain and owls, moss and all the pirates of the shadows are left outside. But when the roof is stolen the universe gets in: skies, branches and stars, and the glassless windows come alive with glimmering leaves.

The wood ended abruptly just beyond Bedham where the path emerged on to a high field which was full of winter turnips and had an abundant view to the west. The path had been ploughed and it petered out after about twenty feet. It continues through a gap in the trees on the other side of the field and skirts the edge of another wood before crossing a road and heading down a bridleway towards the River Arun. I love the paths that run the boundary of woods and fields; they are places where these two very different worlds meet, and now that farmers tend not to plough right up to the hedges any more there are these eight-foot-wide winding swathes which are a much-needed haven for butterflies, voles and wild flowers. I watched as a buzzard lumbered off a tree overhead. Buzzards spend a lot of their time sitting in the highest trees at the edges of woods. I thought for a moment it might have been a red kite as they are moving east from one of their strong-holds on the Downs twenty miles or so to the west just above Petersfield. Red kites have bigger engines than buzzards and perfectly forked tails, their feathers shine, they are glamorous. Buzzards always seem more sullen.

From the field just beyond Springs Farm the view south spreads onto the soft expanse of the Downs. Red admirals and speckled wood butterflies were running another fallow area on the edge of the field. Red admirals are fast flyers: they have intent. They don't float like the speckled woods, who appear to exist only in woodland shafts and pools of light and whose sole purpose is just to dream. Ten minutes later I arrived at the River Arun and sat on the bridge for a while smoking a roll-up and contemplating the idea of a speckled wood butterfly tattoo. An emperor dragonfly joined me, settling on my little blue backpack.

I remember spending one whole day as a child trying to catch one and then crucifying it on a setting board, having ended its life with my mother's nail varnish remover. It was the coloured ranks of emerald greens up against azure blue and the intricate lattice-like brittle wings that were so intoxicat-ing; for a nine-year-old boy it was a triumph to have caught it. Over the next two or three days I watched as the colours faded completely leaving a desolate husk: it was one of too many lessons that taught me to understand the utter foolishness of assuming I could own such a thing. As I have become older the very idea that I could own a tree or a rose or a sheep or a giant panda places me in the same house as the man who sells dead butterflies.

Like the riverbanks, the butterflies of September are quieter, and as there was no one around I thought about taking a swim, but it was so lovely just to sit and watch the dragonflies skidding through the air and the river sliding by. Just up from the river is the Arun canal but it is empty, the base is almost dry and nature is gradually taking it back. I had an idea of following it eastwards to where the path I was meant to be taking crossed over it but in most places it is an impenetrable bowl of tangled branches and brambles so I headed along what I assumed must have been what was left of the towpath.

About half a mile along, standing on the remains of the edge of a crumbling bridge, was an ornamental china shire horse; it still had most of the grey glaze on it. It felt strange that someone had placed it there – a child would have begged to take it home. A little further on from the shire-horse bridge, I cut across a small field, then over a couple of much newer bridges and re-joined the path at Furnacepond Cottages. From there I walked back over the river to a place simply called Haybarn.

The map showed the path cutting down to the left of the barns so I followed it without question; it was bumpy and unkempt and the ground was covered in trailing bramble fronds and the remains of chicken manure. It emerged back onto a half-stony road, but it wasn't until I saw the new-built barns in front me once again that I realised I had taken the wrong path and that it was just luck that had taken me back to where I had made a wrong turn. What was shocking was that before I had seen the barns the path felt completely unfamiliar. In English folklore, and even more so in Irish, this unplanned circular diversion would be put down to the mischief of fairies, who are notorious for leading travellers astray. Perhaps the sweet little elderberries I had eaten along the way had been my undoing and I had to complete a circle and would only be released from the spell once I had passed the place where I had picked them. The other explanation is that since the map has been printed two new barns have been built and rather than the path passing to the left of them it now runs, as I discovered, between them. It carries on over an old wooden footbridge, then across a bumpy field leading to Shipbourne Farm and then on to the Fittleworth Road.

As I headed back to the car, the light breeze and the occasional flurries of sunlight had all but gone, the cloud had thickened and the air underneath it was warm and increasingly still. The road led back into the wood; the same wood from where I had started. The tunnel-coloured entrance stood where the hedges ended and the wood began. Like fields and meadows, woods have wonderful names, Beggars Copse, the Wilderness, Black Acre Forest, Sweet Haws and Treblers Wood. But the wood I started out from and the same wood I entered on my return were two completely different places. I set out in a wood where distinct blocks of light stood alongside the trees, this light had in places shattered into little pieces that hovered over the ground; the air was alive with flies and everything was wet. The wood I entered on my return was damp and still, deep in silence, asleep in a dream.

Change allows us some kind of measure of time, the ability to see, to know the great changes that have taken place in the landscape around us. We mark time with the arrival of motorways, wind turbines and the day when the canal went dry: this is the creation of history and it is so overwhelmingly heavy because it has apparently set solid. But it is also a very limited view of reality. Because in between what I perceive as major changes are millions of minute changes unfolding every second – I exist in the midst of a constant movement of many million realities, colliding, absorbing, becoming. Reality is not fixed it is fluid, what appears static is in fact changing all the time. If I could see all these changes taking place every second Planet Earth would be glittering.

Bedham, West Sussex

Start and finish. OS map 134. Grid reference 024237

Time: four hours

....

▶ Head along the A272 heading west out of Billingshurst
for about three-and-a-half miles until you come to a
crossroads in the middle of a wood: here turn left. The
car park is about 200 yards up on the right. Walk out of
the car park, turn right and take the next right turn up
through Hawkhurst Court.

▶ Once through Hawkhurst Court, follow the path
down into the wood then take the path on your right,
which is halfway up the other side of that little valley.
This path leads through the wood to Bedham. When
you reach the road, turn right and continue walking
through Bedham.

▶ After about a third of a mile there is a well-marked path
on your right. Take this path, which leads up to what
remains of the church of St Michael and All Angels. Just
beyond the church is a minor road: turn left here.

▶ After about 200 yards there is a path on your right. Follow
this path to the end of the wood and across the field at
the top, heading in a south-easterly direction under the
telegraph poles.

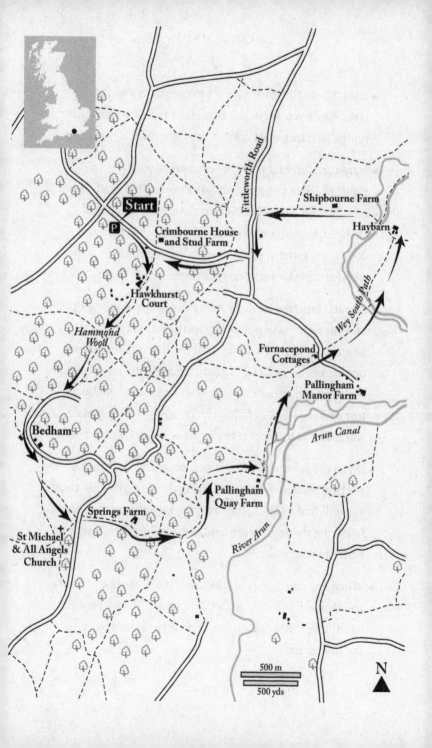

▶ The path on the other side is no more than a gap in the trees. Once you are in the wood take the path immediately on the left; this leads down to a minor road.

▶ Here turn left and take the waymarked path on your right, which is about twenty yards away. This heads down past Springs Farm. Follow it to the corner of the field then through a gate and along the fence line. The path continues in the opposite corner, leading through another wood and past a very pretty cottage.

▶ About a hundred yards beyond the cottage is another path on your right: take it heading north. This path curves around the edge of a field and about half a mile further on you will come to Pallingham Quay Farm and the Arun. Here you can either cross the river and follow the canal tow path, or you can follow the Wey South Path, which will lead you to another bridge some two miles further on.

▶ If you choose to follow the towpath, carry on until you see two bridges on your left. Cross these and beyond them you will find a gate. Climb over the gate and up the bank following the edge of the field, with Pallingham Manor Farm on your right.

▶ When you reach what is effectively the driveway, turn left and this will take you to Furnacepond Cottages: here you join the Wey South Path back across the river and up to the hay barns.

▸ Cut in between the barns and continue along the path, which leads over the dry canal then past Shipbourne Farm on your right, and half a mile further on to a minor road.

▸ Here turn left and after half a mile take the next minor road on your right. This leads you back through the wood to the car park.

Blatherwycke, Northamptonshire

The fish in the grass

Blatherwycke has the feel of the morning after the party, the end of a love affair when the memories of all it was are far more vivid than anything the present reality can muster. This feeling is really compounded by the fact that there appears to be nothing new in Blatherwcyke: nothing has been built recently, it is more of a hamlet than a village and there are more cottages than houses. Up until the end of the Second World War there was a stately home here; there are pictures of it online: a grand block of a grey building set behind a striped mown lawn that leads down to an ornamental circular pond with a fountain in the middle of it. Behind the large rectangular windows must have been dressing tables, cupboards full of clothes, dogs asleep on floors, the adding up of numbers and the chaos love ferments. The family must have fallen on hard times and during the Second World War the house was used as a billet for British and Polish troops. After that it was left empty and finally it was demolished in 1948.

The big house may now be gone but there are bits of it still etched into the land. A delightful bridge spans the southern end of a large blue lake and just beyond where the path begins there is a walled garden and beyond that a large cream-coloured empty stable block. I am sure there must still be people living who can remember going through the front door; as long as something is contained in a living memory, then it still exists. In some religions there is a belief that your spirit does not leave the earth completely until your name is never mentioned again.

I once met an old countryman who told me that the swallows and house martins didn't head south to Africa until the first winds of autumn blew them away. Perhaps it is true. Yesterday they were flying low over the fields, and hurrying through the air and today a wild northerly wind is undoing summer and they have gone: there is not one in the clean sky. Just beyond what was once the immediate boundary of Blatherwycke Hall the path runs underneath a long stand of horse chestnut trees. I love the first winds of autumn, they are usually warm; these are blustery days when the trees are shaken, each gust loosening handfuls of chestnuts, which clatter to the ground bouncing off the earth. There is surely nothing else in the plant world that is quite so varnished as a new horse chestnut.

To the south the land rises gently into a square block of maize which appears to have a statue standing in the middle of it. Above the maize I saw two red kites being danced around by the wind. In the year 2000, thirty red kites from Spain were released in and around Rockingham Forest, which lies on the other side of the lake, and their numbers have swelled considerably since then. Along with many species of animals and birds, red kites were very much casualties of the Tudor vermin laws, which placed a bounty on the heads of sparrows, hedgehogs, polecats, green woodpeckers and many more creatures. In the eighteenth century the head of each decapitated sparrow was worth the equivalent of 1p. It was 5p for foxes and badgers, two and a half pence for a polecat and 2p for each hedgehog head. With an average wage of a few shillings a week many people in the countryside took to killing anything on the vermin list on sight and it has been estimated that a hundred million sparrows were killed between 1700 and 1930.

There must have been at least 2,000 terns and gulls on Blatherwycke Lake, which was glimpsing blue through the chestnut trees and stretching almost into the sky beyond them. It was impossible to distinguish between the two. I would have assumed the birds on the lake were all herring gulls until something disturbed them and they took off in a great flurry. Terns tend to bounce through the air whereas gulls are steadier, especially in the evenings, when they move through the sky without seeming to beat their wings as they haul their way home. Beyond the lake the path runs alongside Willow Brook through a series of fields. For most of the time the brook is hidden behind high hedges but in places the bank is clear and leads down to the running water, which looked as if it might be just perfect for a wild brown trout or two. But the wind was jeering in every direction and this, combined with some hefty rippling, made it pretty much impossible to see into the secrets this brook may keep.

About half a mile before King's Cliffe the path crosses the river over a small wooden bridge sheltered from the wind by trees and hedges on either side; underneath and on both sides of the bridge the surface of the water was undisturbed. Lying on the bed of the brook were curious red patches and ribbons of sunken horse chestnuts; the current wasn't strong enough to move them and they would be there until the brook swells with rain and the flow picks up. I saw the shadow first, almost unmoving on the river bed, stationary brown trout are almost invisible in the water; they become translucent, only giving themselves away when they move. Looking into the water from above the trout and the brook become almost one. Most of the natural world is invisible to us. Just one cupful of this brook water under a microscope would reveal a teeming city of life.

As I walked towards King's Cliffe the wind picked up a little, but the air was fresh and newly made, every leaf was moving, nothing was still and the brittle light cracked every surface and did away with the dust of summer. On the outskirts of the village the path runs alongside some allotments and there was a blast of colours – blue plastic sacks, red-handled rakes and a cascade of orange nasturtiums pouring through the fence. A single allotment is just a vegetable patch, but glue all these vegetable patches together with a scattering of sheds, water butts and various fruit trees in different stages of size and leaf and you end up with a feast of a field. We are used to seeing the mausoleum of monoculture, and yes, there can be beauty in a field of barley when just before it ripens it becomes almost blue. And a field of wheat under an August moon: how the wind turns it to water. But at this time of year the cereal fields are empty: they have given birth, the opera is over and they lie there naked, waiting to be covered by the blankets of winter; the soil is the bed from which everything on land is born. I have no idea how the term 'flower bed' came into being but I am very glad that it did.

Past the allotments, the path heads towards a minor road and nudges up to a house on the corner which was almost surrounded by a battalion of large flowerpots frilling over with begonias. There is something other-worldly about begonias; they seem to be enduring a penance which consists of being planted in rows alongside bungalow driveways. They are actually extraordinarily beautiful – a combination of wax and lace – but there is a sadness about them: each begonia always seems so utterly alone. I was going to take the Jurassic Way, which leads through Westhay Wood, part of Rockingham Forest, but a group of cyclists wheeled past and suddenly I imagined an almost gravelled road heading mostly straight through the trees, a kind of suburban walkway with ditches on either side. The abandoned railway line felt like a good idea, but having gone down the bank to peer under a bridge, I saw it was tangled up with brambles, broken dustbins and the skeletal remains of vacuum cleaners. The alternative was a much smaller green dotted line that led through some fields alongside the edge of Westhay Wood. This didn't look as if it was walked at all, there was no apparent trail laid down by consistent tramping, and the further west it led the more enchanting it did indeed become.

The field boundaries on the map didn't exist on the ground; there must have been hedges here once but all that was left of them were a few old blackthorn trees that had grown out of line. These fields have never been ploughed, mainly because emerging in the middle of two of them is a small stream, an easy source of water for cattle and sheep; smaller fields surrounded by trees tend not to be planted with cereal crops simply because 10 per cent of the growing area is given up to the hunger of shadows. On the southern side of the fields were occasional gates and gaps, perfect frames for holding the distance, an unfolding of misshapen fields, an unordered arrangement of trees and a small fire that occasionally flashed now and then, hunched in next to a hedge – all of this beneath a sky stippled at times with flying leaves. Little of it has perhaps changed in centuries: only the characters that inhabit it are different, and the coming and going of generations of swallows and flies, rabbits and kestrels.

Since there was no path, I headed for the corner of the field and entered a different world. The trees in this section of Rockingham Forest had been thinned and the canopy was wide open in places, letting the light in, but the noise of the wind was no longer around me – it was above me. A couple of yards beyond the field is a discernible trail which meanders and flows around trees with no apparent purpose; woods are networked with paths, most of which we cannot see.

Human beings are not the only species to make paths. The slopes of the Downs in southern England where I live are rippled with sheep paths running horizontally along the sides of even the steepest slopes. Sheep will also make paths across fields leading to water troughs and hay stalls, and these paths are just wide enough for one animal. Ants lay down scent trails, which very quickly become cleared walkways with ants heading towards the nest using one side and those heading away using the other. The rainforests of central Africa are ribboned with a network of huge walkways cleared through the dense undergrowth: these were created by elephants and many of them have been used for generations.

Deer create wonderfully sleek and flowing paths through woodland, but these can be hard to find; the best place to pick them up is next to a stream or a ditch where they have left their hoof prints, their sign in the mud. Deer are secretive, but following these paths can sometimes lead you to the clearings tucked in under the low-hanging branches of large trees: this is where they sleep, leaving some of their hair on the smoothed ground. Once when I was walking through a wood in Buckinghamshire I became aware that I was being watched so I stopped and listened intently. It was mid-November and I was on a path sunk between two steep banks, a naturally vulnerable place to be. It must have taken about a minute before I could actually see who was observing me. They were hidden in their own stillness, thirty to forty fallow deer standing motionless within the trees, staring directly at me. It was only when I looked back into their eyes that the spell of camouflage was broken – then suddenly and simultaneously they broke cover and set off in one movement, one flurry with one sound. In no more than five seconds they were all gone. How many times have I walked through a herd of deer without even knowing they were there?

The path leading into Rockingham Forest looked as if it had been created by children; as if there should be a camp at the end of it made of sticks and reeds, but I knew it led to the embankment of the abandoned railway. On the map the wider feathering around the route of a railway line indicates the steepness of the embankments leading down to it and this was almost a canyon, a dark depth which would have had just an hour or two of sunlight a day, a place that was permanently damp. This was the point where I intended to head north and cut through the forest until I reached the Jurassic Way, but running along the edge of the embankment was a trail, a thread through the trees. It leads past broken bridges and the remains of a fence and tiptoes along until it emerges almost through a hedge onto the Jurassic Way, which was everything I hoped it wouldn't be: a wide, machine-made swathe.

Really, it was a road – neat, ordered, blunt – but floating through the trees was an aroma that is undeniably delicious. Wild mushrooms are the flowers of autumn. There had been a few field mushrooms in the stream fields but they were very much past their sell-by date, they looked drenched and ragged. The scent coming through the trees was thick and fecund, a mixture of yeast, sweat, almonds, mud and molasses. Barging up through the grass in the wood were vivid stands of fly agaric mushrooms, and where there are fly agarics there can be ceps (or penny buns), as they belong to the same family – and ceps are worth forging rivers for. I once had soup made entirely from ceps in Lithuania; it was served in a hollowed-out loaf.

And as the soup was drunk the idea was to break off little pieces of bread and dip it in, this was a meal that warmed every part of you.

Whereas a soup made from the red-and-white spotted fly agaric would induce hallucination and possibly euphoria, along with a high chance of death. Shamen in the Arctic dry the mushrooms and peel off the surface layers, then steep them in boiling water and drink it as tea as, so it is said, did the Vikings before they went into battle. The association between fly agaric mushroom and the fairy world comes from the experience of having ingested them. The mushrooms loosen the ropes of hard reality, softening the vehemence of time, opening doors in the walls we place around our own dark canyons and intoxicating the sentries that patrol the boundaries of all we consider to be beautiful. What they do not do is show us a different world: they just show us this world differently.

Despite hunting around for a good fifteen minutes there was not a cep to be seen. Ambling along the Jurassic Way were three forest wardens, all wearing identical green and purple fleeces. 'Are there cep in these woods?' I asked. 'Yes, there are,' they replied. I had a feeling they knew where the cep might be, followed by another feeling I understood completely: that they weren't going to tell me.

The Forest Lodge is not hard to find; it lies on the Jurassic Way on the edge of Rockingham Forest. Along with a bicycle hire centre and an outdoor clothing shop and a few lonely notice boards there is also a café that echoes, but really the whole place feels like the reception area of an airport hotel: the only thing that was missing was a line of flagpoles. It was the dissonance that was so shocking: there was nothing celebrating what was on the outside on the inside. Maybe I am a fool for imagining an open fire, nest boxes on the walls, crab apple jelly on toast, elderberry wine, pine needle tea – but I fear it is just cheaper to import mango smoothies, prawn cocktail flavoured crisps and Colombian coffee.

The walk from the Lodge back to Blatherwycke goes up and down through fields, over several streams and through little copses and wanders past a large house that sits behind a small lake holding a square jetty on which were two empty sun loungers. On the south side of Blatherwycke Lake hundreds of pink-footed geese had settled on an uncut field; geese move very slowly across the ground, as if they are constantly trying to retain their balance. Just before I reached the road a cormorant flew across the sky. Cormorants have taken to coming inland and helping themselves to all the generously stocked fishing lakes; it always feels strange to see them so far from the sea. But nowhere in Britain is more than seventy-two miles from the sea. This is a maritime island and whilst we may call it dry land Britain can hardly be described as dry. The paths are muddy for at least six months of the year and the grass is wet for much of the same time and although it has taken 6,000 years to cut down the woodland that once covered these islands it has also taken that amount of time to drain them. We should perhaps now leave the meres and marshes that remain, the great stands of reeds and swaying sedges. I am not sure if anyone has ever added up the ditches, dykes and drains in miles, but when you combine these with every stream and every river it will illuminate the fact that we live on a series of little islands surrounded by moats of water. This has been a walk through water as much as through land and it is this constant proximity of the water to the land that ferments such a rich intermingling of light and life, of gulls and goldfinches, cormorants and kestrels. This may be one of the greenest lands in the world but it is also one of the bluest as well.

— ◦ —

Blatherwycke, Northamptonshire

Start and finish: OS map 234. Grid reference 972963
Time: three hours

▶ I parked just beyond the bridge in Blatherwycke, as the walk begins at the entrance to what was Blatherwycke Hall. Follow this path east, past the edge of the lake and then along the brook through several fields until you come to a small bridge.

▶ Once over the bridge, the path continues into King's Cliffe. Pass the allotments, turn left and follow what is no more than a track up to the road; cross over and continue heading north until you reach an old railway bridge.

▶ On the other side of this bridge, turn left and continue walking through the fields until you meet the wood: the path into the wood starts in the top right-hand corner. Follow this path until it reaches the edge of the old railway

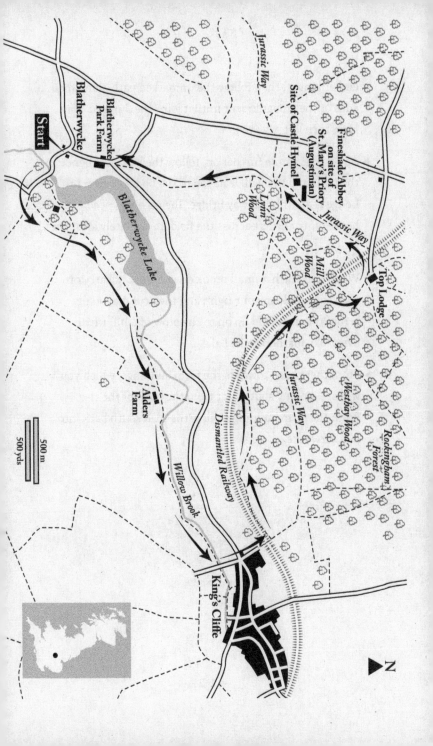

embankment, then follow the unmarked path along the edge of the embankment until it joins the Jurassic Way. Here turn left.

▶ About half a mile further on, follow the Way as it bends to the right and this will lead you to the Lodge. Beyond the Lodge is another railway bridge. The path you need to take heads off to the left across the field immediately after the bridge.

▶ When you reach a small brook do not cross it: carry on, with the brook on your right, and then cut diagonally across the next field up on to the brow of a hill which overlooks Blatherwycke Lake.

▶ From there head towards the farm buildings, which you will see looking south-east from the brow of the rise. From the farm buildings follow the road south back into Blatherwycke.

The Chutes, Wiltshire

The day after the storm

The climate of Planet Earth is unstable. It is this instability that gives its infinite variation. Rains arrive, rains fail, pressure systems constantly dissipate and combine, the temperature rockets and plummets, the land freezes, the land thaws. Only in the tropics, and only then at certain times of year, does it rain every day at four o'clock in the afternoon.

Three thousand miles north of the tropic of Capricorn on the relatively small temperate island of Britain, the first day of November is always different from the one that went before it. Usually by this time of year low pressure systems begin queuing up over the Atlantic Ocean, then blow in one after another. The isobars tighten and when they do the wind becomes stronger; and once every twenty or thirty years a great hulk of a low-pressure system arrives with the isobars packed as tight as tree rings, and then there is a storm to remember. Yesterday the sea from the top of the Downs was a moving mass of white and grey; and I could taste the salt spray that was being blown inland from four miles away and watch the almost static red light of the search helicopter sent out to try to find a fourteen-year-old boy who had been swept off the rocks into waves that would have broken oak trees.

Today, the day after the storm, the minor road leading into Lower Chute was sprinkled with sticks and rendered with coloured leaves; it was almost beautiful, but the trees above the road looked exhausted, especially the ashes, which were greying and tattered. I walked west from the Hatchet Inn out of Lower Chute, where the land rises to the brow of a small hill. The path hadn't been walked since the storm, there were no footprints and the mud had turned to slurry; really there wasn't a grain of soil left that could absorb any more water, and neither could the air. Just above the village where the land opens out to the south, the view blurred, the mist absorbing the distance, clinging in auras around clumps of trees and wallowing in low-lying fields; it was what the Irish would call a 'soft' morning. But with no rain and barely a breeze, the birds were out and about feeding on the bounty left behind by the high winds.

During the storm the rooks and the gulls were being blown around like litter, but what about the smaller birds – wrens, blue tits and hedge sparrows – where did they go and where do they sleep? Every night in this country over a hundred million birds go to sleep and really none of us knows where. Just before walking into Upper Chute I passed a pair of pied wagtails foraging along the edges of pools that had formed in a field of winter barley. They are constantly busy birds. The British pied wagtail is actually a subspecies of the Continental white wagtail. In the countryside they are still known as water wagtails and there are far more of them than their yellow and grey cousins. I have always thought the grey wagtail has been rather short-changed on the name front. It is true that it is slightly less yellow than the yellow wagtail but with a slate blue back along with a bright yellow breast it can hardly be described as grey.

Upper Chute seemed in lockdown; there was nobody out and not one car drove through. On a clear day the pub on the edge of the village would have had a view to serenade a pint or two but today the place was empty and with the heavy air muffling the sound it was completely quiet. The track beyond the village rises and falls through a series of valleys edged with woods and uneven fields. Just beyond Deans Farm a man wearing a thick jacket was cutting back brambles and mending a fence enclosing a pony paddock. We said good morning, agreed it had been quite a storm and he carried on working while telling me he enjoyed the frosty mornings best of all. Walking away it struck me that I had never thought about having a favourite morning although the mornings in the Australian outback rank highly, the red earth, the sun sliding through the eucalyptus trees as the heat releases their scent – as the Aboriginal people will tell you, it is a dream, but no more of a dream than a heavily grey autumn morning where the mist leaches the colours out of the fields and woods of southern England. As the path headed north along a rising ridge there was no escaping the grip of the thickening mist burying the trees and the destination of the hedgerows. It began to thin just before New Zealand Farm and as it did the first drips of rain started falling. By the time the path reached the road it was falling quite heavily: I love walking in the rain.

Rather strangely, the house next to the path leading down to Hippenscombe Bottom isn't marked on the map. Walking up through the woods next to the house was a young couple and with them were a small grey dog holding a red ball in its mouth, and a black cat with a pink collar. We said good morning. I asked whether the cat had been walking with them. The young woman replied that it had – they had just walked two miles together. I used to look after a walking cat called Dusty, she would mosey down the road with me to the pub, where she would lie in front of the fire and terrorise the dogs. Whenever I visited the village shop she tagged along and occasionally we ventured slightly further beyond the village out towards the fields hugging the bottom of the Downs. In the most recent edition of *The Barefoot Diaries* Jackie Morris, who lives in Pembrokeshire, writes: 'Walking with dogs is so very different to walking with cats, the cats taught me to slow down, to look, to stop.' I asked the young woman what happened when other walkers approached with dogs and she said the cat would simply slip away and hide in a swathe of long grass or slink into a bush until the dogs had passed. Cats sleep for sixteen hours a day, they are asleep for two-thirds of their life, and until I started walking with Dusty I had no idea that their natural pace is also soporific. They really do amble and dawdle, they bumble along and delightfully have no concept of being in a hurry: they are not subjected by the dark mantra repeating and repeating *time is money*.

By the time we had finished talking the rain was well and truly falling. It wasn't heavy – downpours make such a wonderful noise – but the wood behind the house was ticking loudly as the droplets hit the leaves and scattered in pearls in the unkempt grass leading into Hippenscombe Bottom. In the chalk hills of southern England valley floors are called 'Bottoms', this purely practical soubriquet just happens to sit well in one of the most sensual landscapes in the world.

Hippenscombe Bottom was carved out by a river of meltwater during the end of the last Ice Age. It bends and turns like a river does: slowly. As you walk down between the high-sided slopes, it is impossible not to feel the residue of the great forces that created it; it reawakens the reality that 14,000 years ago some ten miles north of here stood a cliff of an ice sheet more than 300 feet high. As the ice retreated, animals, birds and insects began to re-colonise these lands and by the time the first human beings returned to this valley it would have been home to cave lions, wolverines, lynx and antelopes.

Now, though, it feels empty. That feeling may have been compounded by the steady rain that encouraged me into a small conifer thicket to pull on some waterproof trousers. I leaned up against one of the trees and lit a cigarette. Being alone in the rain always raises the intensity of existence. Perhaps the reason why Hippenscombe Bottom feels so separate is that up until quite recently it was. All those who lived here were outside the jurisdiction of the civil parish system, they did not come under the authority of the Church of England.

These little pockets of land were known as 'extra-parochial': beyond the reach of religion, here they had no church and no priests; they existed beyond the reach of religion, which meant that those living here before 1857 paid no tithes, they also received no poor relief either. In the records I could find it states that the inhabitants of these places 'relieved their own poor'. The names of some of the settlements that evolved in these extra-parochial parcels of land clearly reveal how they were viewed by the rest of the population; my favourite, I think, is an area of land called 'Nowhere', which is in Norfolk.

After about a mile, this valley in Wiltshire straightens and widens out considerably, the path leads gently down towards some houses and farm buildings and the spell of the Ice Age is broken, but even in the rain it didn't really feel part of England. Maybe it was the large modern white house surrounded by cropped balls of privet growing in large pots and the expanse of umber coloured pasture leading up to it and the path, which was more of a dirt road, heading towards it that gave it the feel of an Australian sheep station. All that was missing was blue sky along with a wind pump placed on top of a white- painted wooden tower – and of course the attention of legions of flies. From the moment I approached the house to the moment I was well beyond this little hamlet a dog, sensing my presence, continued to bark, but apart from that I neither heard nor saw another soul.

The path leading out of Hippenscombe Bottom rises steeply upward along a trammelled and rutted track along the edge of a large copse. About a hundred and fifty years ago someone planted a line of beech saplings which have now grown into an almost rhino grey wall of tree trunks. They perhaps had been planted to protect a hazel coppice that still sits behind them from the westerly winds that whip over these slopes at this time of year. The straight sticks of hazel, known as rods, are still used by the very few individuals who still know how to lay and train a hedge but gardeners pretty much gave them up long ago in favour of bamboo canes, which are less bulky and last a little longer. Most of the hazelnuts have gone by this time of year; there were just one or two left hanging on the ends of the branches that wouldn't take the weight of the grey squirrels, who by now had eaten and buried all those they could reach. Despite the copious quantities of hazelnut shells covering the ground, when I looked up into the trees I couldn't spot a single drey – the nests made of leaves and grass that squirrels build to sleep out their hibernation. I remember seeing many of them as a child, great bundles of leaves wedged into the forks of trees, but they have almost vanished from the woods now. In the last twenty years squirrels have either adapted to the British winter, or the winters are no longer cold enough to warrant hibernation. At a talk I attended last week on geo-engineering – which is the term used for the emerging science of 'climate control' – all four professors were of one mind: the planet is warming. Yes: global warming is going to reframe how everything lives on Planet Earth, but whilst that is going to pose some huge problems, the biggest problem of all is human behaviour and all that we have put in place that we currently believe is defining progress. Most climate scientists now agree that the number and intensity of severe storms hitting these shores is set to increase. What I say is that they will keep coming until they have cracked the template from which they have risen.

A huge broken limb of a sycamore lay across the path. It was just beyond the brow of the hill. The rest of the tree had lost half of its mass. The falling branch had also brought down some smaller trees, their sapling trunks stood at the side of the path jagged and tattered. Just like us, the outside of trees gives no indication as to the inside. Bark is really just skin, the skin of the tree. Trees are the midwives of life, feeding and protecting, in some cases, hundreds of different species, of which we are just one. The wood behind the bark has its own particular texture and colour, depending on the species: hardwoods tend to be darker than softwoods, and sycamore wood is a rich cream almost the same colour as ewes' colostrum, the first milk they produce to feed their lambs.

Another large branch had fallen on to the path about 200 yards before I was due to cross the road; this one was an ash. Ash wood is one of the whiter woods, and it is also one of the only two woods – along with silver birch – that burns well directly after cutting: neither of them need seasoning. It was only when I ventured into the wood to walk round the impassable branch lying across the path that the true force of the storm became apparent. Apart from many broken branches on the ground a beech tree had snapped halfway up its trunk and was lying horizontally suspended in the limbs of the trees next to it. It must have stopped raining as I was walking towards the road. It was hard to tell, as the wood was still dripping, but the birds started singing and they don't tend to sing in the rain, simply because their songs are dampened when it is raining. But it is lovely to hear them at this particular point announcing that the rain has passed and knowing that nature celebrates this in song.

Chute Causeway lies right on the brow of the hill: it is a minor road that was once a major road. It is simply marked on the map as a Roman road. These are usually fabulously straight but this one bends and turns as it travels along the top of this ridge of chalk. The path on the other side of the road leads gently downhill, passing between Bottomhalves Copse and Mafeking Clump, and running the entire length of it is a telegraph line which despite being almost pulled to the ground by several large fallen branches miraculously seemed to have remained in one piece. At the end of the path there is another tightly packed stand of beech trees running from east to west. On the ground beneath them was a lake of coppery coloured leaves: in the midst of all that was destroyed and torn, here was a newly made temple of peace.

At the heart of Chute Standen stands a lone sweet chestnut tree. Sweet chestnut trees were introduced by the Romans, along with rabbits and pheasants, whilst the sycamore was introduced from southern Europe in the Middle Ages. Extracting the sweet chestnuts from their pincushion casings by hand is always going to end up in bleeding fingers: the best way to do it is to roll them over a hard surface underfoot, which pops them out of their fierce shells.

Having gathered half a pound or so of this delicious bounty, I set off along the minor road leading back into Lower Chute. The sky was easing, the distance opening, the air drying a little in a light breeze. Could this be a combination the geo-engineers would programme? Would we be subjected to perfect summers and rains that fell only between one o'clock and four o'clock in the morning? Would we have cold winters and sharp frosts – bearing in mind that without them the bluebells would not flower – and what would be the maximum allowable wind speed? We could have a white Christmas every year and Tunbridge Wells could become a tropical paradise. The very idea that there is something real called 'good weather' is very flawed. Yes, there is warm weather; there is wet weather and cold weather and once in a while, for the time being at least, there is a great storm – but a wet day is surely no worse than a sunny day. It may be slightly less comfortable but it is no less beautiful.

Storms are nature's reapers, challenging, taunting, pressing, testing all that lives under the illusion of permanence. The purpose of storms is to create space for new life, for new shapes, new combinations of colour; they create natural crises: storms are creators of change. The very idea that I should choose certainty, a stormless world, over uncertainty means I have quietly crept into a box not understanding that I have no intrinsic right to my next breath, but storms also hold another secret.

Once, about fifteen years ago, I was walking in Snowdonia with some friends. We were scrambling up the north side of the Carnedds, which rise to over 3,000 feet on the east side of Mount Snowdon. I could see the clouds travelling over the sky at great speed above me but the slope was in the lee of the wind. The moment I clambered on to the ridge the noise was almost overwhelming, it was like stumbling into thunder. The force of the gusts were so strong I couldn't stand so I crawled across the rocks into a small round roofless windbreak, I lay there alone in the midst of the storm, where I found a peace I had never known before.

The Chutes, Wiltshire

Start and finish: OS map 131. Grid reference 310533
Time: three hours

▶ From the Hatchet Inn in Lower Chute take the road that heads uphill in front of it. Halfway up the hill there is a waymarked path on your right: take it. This heads behind some houses and out over a field.

▶ When you reach the minor road, turn left and follow it through Upper Chute. The road ends just beyond the pub, where the path begins. Follow this path until you can see the pylons in front of you from the brow of a rise: here turn right and follow the path up to Chantry Buildings.

▶ The path continues north until it reaches an old hedge line which has now become almost a line of trees: here turn left and follow the path to just before New Zealand Farm. Here, you need to take what is effectively the farm's driveway, which will lead you to the minor road, Chute Causeway.

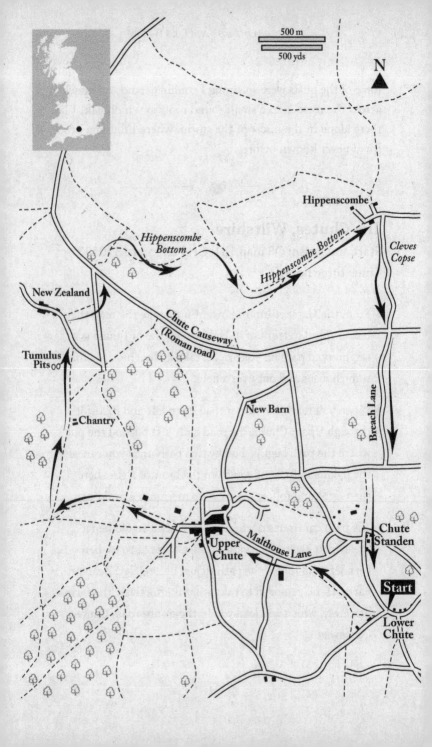

► Pick up the path on the opposite side of Chute Causeway and follow it down through a small wood to Hippenscombe Bottom. The path then continues eastwards all the way into the tiny hamlet of Hippenscombe.

► Just beyond Hippenscombe hamlet you will need to take the path heading south, which rises steeply up the side of the hill. This path leads to the road, where you take the path heading down, which is immediately opposite.

► At the end of this path turn right and some 400 yards further on take the path on your left: this will lead you into Chute Standen. From here follow the minor road south into Lower Chute.

Damsons and dust

By mid-November the sky is beginning to sink; it has, on most days, lost its brilliant blue and the clouds are truly growling, hunting down the last of the year's remaining flowers. In West Wales the air was grey and gluey, holding all the mustard-coloured trees under siege and bringing the black slate graveyards into bloom. I love autumn, it slides in so very gently, offering damsons and rose hips in exchange for a tender decay. By the time the red garlands of bryony arrive, which is when the old man's beard is beginning to turn the hedges into foam, what was tender has toughened, what was warm becomes cold, and when the weak sun goes down a thick and beautiful gloom sets in.

It was a classic November day. It wasn't warm and it wasn't cold, the sky was grey but not heavy enough for real rain; occasionally there were a few drops but nothing to put on a waterproof for. At about 1.45, I left the car parked in between

Trefilan school, which has only fifteen pupils, and the church whose name I couldn't read because someone had placed a black bin liner over the noticeboard. As I set off down the little road past a barn which was the size and proportions of a small cottage, I couldn't know I would be cutting it short. The ford beyond the barn bubbled and swayed over the road; it was too deep to wade in walking boots, but there was a footbridge and on the other side of it, perched almost next to the running water, was a strange green corrugated iron building half the size of a garage, yet it didn't seem like a shed.

Cowering in the hedge on the other side of the ford were three pink campion flowers dressed in vivid pink, but the party was over, all the other guests had long gone, they were alone, with all the bees tucked inside their cities now, their nectar would go undrunk and their seed unknown. It is said that in their lifetime each worker bee harvests one teaspoonful of honey from orchards, gardens and meadows and that it takes 55,000 miles of flight to harvest one pound of honey.

The meadows just beyond Sychpant Farm were dented by hoof prints and the grass was lying flat on the ground. There was absolutely no indication that I was walking a path across these fields, none of the grass had been trodden into a trail of any kind. In the absence of a marked path to follow, it is the landmarks of woods, copses and isolated houses that become the compass and, to begin with at least, it took more time to walk between A and B simply because I was spending so much time looking at the map and the land, and dealing with my fear of trespassing.

It took me a while to reach the minor road where the walk swings left up the driveway to Pentre Farm. Here I spent ten minutes or so scouring the hedges for any signs of a path beyond them. Eventually I worked out that the path leads through the middle of the garden of the house opposite the farm. Many footpaths pass through farmyards but I have never walked through the middle of someone's garden before and here the feeling of trespass became almost overwhelming. It was a public path going through a very private space, leading past evenly placed wellington boots and empty boxes, a half-weeded flower bed with a fork standing upright at the edge of it, and the remains of summer – chairs and benches and a large beach umbrella stacked under an open-sided shed. But what if it wasn't the path after all and, of course, what if I roused a sleeping Rottweiler? At the back of the garden, however, there is a gate, and on the gate is a very public yellow-and-black notice that reads 'Beware of the Bull'.

Bullshit is a little different from cow shit. First of all there is much more of it. Bulls can produce cowpats the size of dustbin lids – either that or a fair smattering of the same shit over a wider area – and it was this that was clearly in the field and it was fresh. First of all, it is never ever a good idea to walk through a field with a loose bull in it, and secondly here someone was asking for trouble by putting a bull in a field that had a public footpath right across the middle of it. Dairy bulls such as Guernseys and Friesians tend to be a great deal more dangerous than beef bulls such as Herefords and Black Angus, but – whatever the breed – if the sign reads 'Beware of the Bull' it needs to be taken seriously.

On the other side of the field was a bridge across the River Aeron. Looking around I couldn't see any cattle but there were dips and of course I couldn't see down to the riverbank. I shouted out and nothing showed, and after ten minutes I decided to cross. The best thing to do would have been to follow the fence line so that if things did get sticky I could just skin the fence, but the river wasn't fenced so slowly and quietly I walked across.

On the other side of the bridge the path leads through another garden, then curves upwards on to a minor road. The road was the only surface that hadn't been softened by water; the fields were drenched and every ditch was running. In the river valley especially there was the constant movement and flow of little rivers and the grey mirrors of pools. There were also birds everywhere – blue tits, great tits, song thrushes, robins, blackbirds and pied wagtails. Whilst they are not uncommon, here there was an abundance of them, and it was not just their company, it was their energy that was so delightful – ceaselessly bright and lively. There is no sense that birds seem to endure the greyest of days as we do.

The road leads on to Abermeurig, where the chapel had come to the end of enduring: there was a 'For Sale' sign attached to the gate by the side of the road. Plaster was falling off the walls in abstract patches but it was really the windows that were dulled with dust and cobwebs that signified no one had looked out of them for quite some time; that, like the campion in the hedge by the ford, the conception of seeds had failed. It is the imagination that is so wounded by the decline of optimism.

The grass was still being cut so I wandered through the gate. The chapel door wasn't locked, it was broken. I gave it a push and painfully it opened, revealing a darkening corridor and a battered chair. I stepped inside. The floorboards were in pieces in the first room and the fireplace was leaning off the wall, but once upon a time with the fire going it must have been snug under its low ceiling. The other two rooms were in much the same state, although the floor wasn't quite so broken. Walking back down the corridor I went through another door, which led into the chapel with its rows of pews. A pulpit took centre stage up against the west wall but most of all there was a complete absence of colour. All the marble plaques had been removed and leaned up against each other in a huddle on the floor. I didn't feel the need to read them; I didn't want to think about the hands that made them, the love that had commissioned them, the incredible narratives of their lives, or that these names that will now dissolve into the unknown, into absolute stillness. Once outside the door at the end of the service the minister shook hands and joked with all who came, while children ran to and fro across the grass and no one then could ever have dreamed this: the day the music died. The Mayans understood that praise and grief are attached to the same root; that any one of us who dares to love, to be swept away, will at some point find themselves in the sea of tears.

On the other side of the chapel, the path enters a wood and strains steeply uphill, running alongside a rushing white stream. It emerges in a farmyard at the top where a cat sat with its back to me on the autum coloured concrete; there was no one else about. From the field beyond the farm it is possible to see most of the valley land and the descending line of Tychryg Hill, to see the walk from above, the woods and the bluffs. Whilst all maps have a scale – one inch to one mile, one centimetre to one kilometre – this scale relates to the distance over the ground. I often wonder just how far above the land I have to be in order to see it at one inch/one per mile. The first map-makers were surely the first human beings to see the land from the air. But it is always wise, I think, to take a look – if the land allows – at where you are heading.

In the corner of the field beyond the farm is a stile which leads across a fence into another piece of woodland but the path beyond it is incoherent, brambled and utterly untrodden. It is meant to lead back to the road. Half a mile along it cuts down between two hedges and becomes a quagmire, which slowly firms into a delightful holloway that winds down to a stream then up again towards Ty'n-y-fron. Approaching the house, I could see a woman unpacking a car, a Dalmatian, and what seemed to be an elderly red setter ambling towards me. She looked up in my direction and half shouted, 'I've changed my shift – I moved it till five.' Before I could think of something to say she carried on: 'Did you hear me, Andrew? I'm going in at five.' 'I'm not Andrew,' I said loudly, then added, 'but he must be a very good looking bloke.' She looked a little startled, then replied, 'No, he just has long hair and jeans' – not that I was wearing jeans – and that was it: she turned and headed for the front door, no wry smile or glint of a grin.

The fish in the small garden pond next to the drive leading out of Llywn-Madoc, the house to the west of Ty'n-y-fron, looked a good deal more pleased to see me; they clustered together, opening their round mouths hoping for food. They weren't so big but they were beautifully coloured mixtures of white and orange, black and red, and once they realised I had nothing to give them they relaxed and returned to suspension.

The naturalist Chris Packham has said that it is the countless garden ponds that have been the saviours of newts, toads, frogs and dragonfly and damsel larvae but the combination of gardens and water runs much deeper than that. Water and land speak a different languages. In dreams, water is the window through which we see and know emotion and eroticism, it invites us to go deeper into the world of feelings. The first dream that I remember having as a child was one in which I was underwater, in the pond. I could see the sunlight on the surface of the water above me and a few small bright green fronds of weed around me; I felt completely weightless and warm and in front of me was the most orange fish I have ever seen. I had reached an age – I must have been about four or five – when, I would imagine, children begin to know and own their own emotions as theirs alone and can draw on those feelings, which begin for each of us to form the heart of every individual experience. As human beings we are born fluent in feeling. Our feelings are there long before we can form words and long before we come under the spell of numbers.

The barn beyond Llywn-Madoc house is in two portions and is fabulously dishevelled and half buried in great piles of manure. A host of sparrows took off in a flurry from one roof, then landed on the other. I love the way they row and how all of them are angry at the same time, with every one of them yelling at the others at once – and just when it seems to be calming down one of them chips in and it all kicks off again.

The sky too was beginning to brood above the path leading round the side of a hill. It was four o'clock and the air was darkening by the minute. The path leading up through the wood looked so delicious with great grey beeches on either side; it was almost night in there so there was no time to go that way and I continued down towards a spring that was marked on the map just in front of Trefran Farm. I was expecting a small, bubbling pool but it was a great grey ragged pond with no apparent movement: the water must leach slowly upwards and it, too, was beginning to darken. It is always the valleys that begin to darken first; up on the hills the end of the day lasts a little longer, so I hurried up the other side of the valley through College Farm and past the small farmhouse built with big stones, and everything seemed quiet and content. As the breeze relaxed there was almost a hint of yellow in the sky; it is only in the autumn and winter that the sky can become infused with lemon yellow at the end of the day.

In the woods behind the farm it was dusk, yet out in the open there was still enough light to just about see the map but I was lost by then: I had followed a farm track assuming it was the path but it petered out in front of a gate over which was a whitening field and at the upper end the silhouettes of leafless elder trees and behind them, just visible, the top of a single telegraph pole jutting out over the horizon of Tychryg

Hill. During the dusk, green turns almost white for about ten minutes or so before sinking into grey and vanishing altogether.

In the upper corner of the field I could see the valley and the houses and farms; it is strange how electric light appears almost orange from a distance. I skinned the fence and then jogged down through a gap in a hedge and rolled under an electric fence on the other side of it; I stopped and took my bearings. In the corner of the field beyond the one I was in I could just make out two flattened tracks in the grass; they had been made by a quad bike and five minutes later I would not have been able to see them. Without the map our senses really kick in, awareness heightens, sight, sound, scent ... what is happening at that point is that I have to read the land, not a printed impression of it. On the one hand it makes me a great deal more vulnerable but on the other so much more alive, yet what is so remarkable is that this happens naturally, that it is hard wired deep within us and when this hard wiring fires up you can feel it rushing in. It is just that what comes with apparent civilisation is a network of roads and millions of signposts telling us all the time where we are. This seems like a knowing, but in fact it has become just as much a forgetting.

The impressions in the grass led to another track, which travelled across the side of Tychryg Hill past some cattle troughs and on to Tal-fan Farm, which is perched above the school and the church. The farmer was crossing the yard as I approached. I said 'Good evening' and asked whether many walkers used the path. 'No, hardly a soul. Well, maybe one or two,' he replied – then he carried on towards a barn in a brittle electric light. By the time I reached the car it was well and truly dark. It is a relief to have a key to turn, which starts an engine, which takes me down roads and into towns and bars and beds, but in the absence of maps and roads, gates and signposts I am not lost. I simply need to find what I left behind in the wilderness.

Tychryg Hill, West Wales

Start and finish: OS map 199. Grid reference 552572
Time: four hours

▶ There is ample room to park next to the church in Trefilan. From there head west along the minor road and, once over the ford, head right along the track up to Sychpant Farm. I jumped the gate and followed the farm track that runs in front of the farm: this leads to a field where the path effectively joins the Aberaeron to Lampeter trail.

▶ The trail leads diagonally over the field and then across another one to just behind Tynparc Cottage before joining what is the driveway, which leads down to a minor road.

▶ Once you reach this road turn right and then take the first left, which leads up to Pentre Farm. Here the path cuts through the back garden of one of the houses, then runs across a field and over the River Aeron, then through another garden and on up to the road.

► When you reach the road turn left and continue on to Abermeurig Chapel. Take the path on your right directly past the chapel and carry on to the top of the hill and through Pen-lan farmyard, then cut diagonally down over the next field and over the stile in the corner and back to the road, where you should turn right.

► Carry on for about half a mile and then take the path on your left, which is to the side of a couple of cottages. This path leads down to the valley floor, over a stream and then up to the driveway of Ty'n-y-fron Farm. Here you should turn left, walking past the house and, beyond it, Llywn Madog.

► Just after Llywn Madog the path turns sharp left and then bears right to some abandoned barns. Stay on the north side of the hedge above the barns and follow the hedge round to the corner of the field and then beyond, keeping the wood on your right. I could see no sign of the path that cuts down from the wood to the spring so I just crossed the field and hopped over a gate, walking past Trefran Farm and down to the road.

► Here you should turn left. After about 200 yards take the path on your right, which leads through College Farm and on up to Pelancwnlle Farm, which is on the brow of the hill. Here take the path heading west across the brow down to Tal-fan Farm and then follow the driveway back to the car.

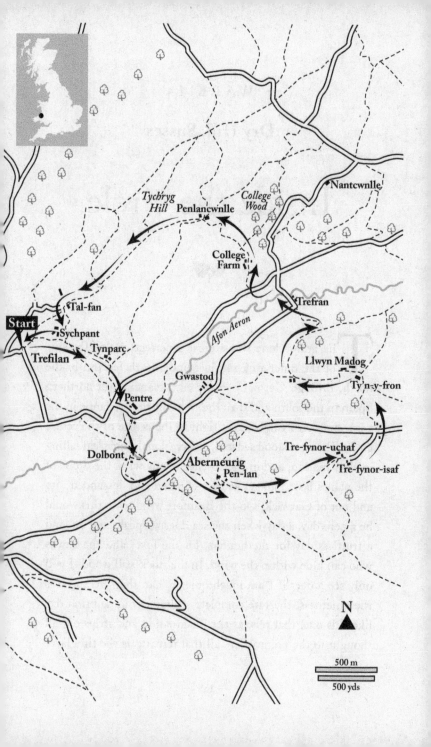

Dry Hill, Sussex

Inside the circle

The anticyclone was almost a perfect circle. The line of the outer ring ran just underneath Iceland in the north, through Germany in the east, glancing off northern Spain in the south and then round to the mid-Atlantic in the west. Southern England sat right in the centre of the centre circle. The trees stood sedated, an occasional single leaf falling in slow motion, and in the absence of any wind the drone of the planes lasted longer as they climbed and descended into and out of Gatwick. On the Beaufort wind scale this would be a zero day, a day when the sea doesn't speak; and on land a fruitless day for the hunters, for the foxes and the hawks who can hide within the wind. In the stock-still woods I will only see a deer if I am much quieter than they are and it is the quietness, the rare complete stillness of an autumn day like this one, that relaxes the imagination and strips out all thought to the point where all that remains is the thin layer of each mortal breath. The centre circles of large anticyclones lie just beyond the reach of the tyranny of time; in the still centre there is only the present moment.

I was met with the tyranny of fences. What would originally have been a path between fields had become an enclosed walkway, a single file between two fences, a mean line on which it is not possible to walk arm in arm with another. Thankfully, this doesn't happen that often, most landowners are not inclined to encase the footpath behind barbed wire.

The incarceration only lasted for a couple of hundred yards, after which the route turns on to what is effectively the driveway leading up to Burnt Pit Farm. As I was wandering up towards the farm a mature South Down ewe came up to the fence and started bleating; she must have been hand-reared as she didn't mind being stroked, and she followed me rather mournfully on the other side of the fence to the field boundary. Lambing time in any flock always bequeaths a handful of orphans. Some have lost their mothers and some are simply not wanted or cared for. I worked as a shepherd as a young man, and still do so for a couple of weeks each spring. Orphan lambs need feeding four or five times every twenty-four hours to begin with; as they grow in strength they can down a litre of milk in about a minute, their whole body punching up on the bottle. Hand-reared sheep never really fit in with the flock, they never quite lose the imprint of their human foster parents, it leaves them not belonging to either. Really we don't do it that well. You see, lambing time is so busy and as a shepherd you get so tired that morning becomes night and time starts to fray. And I see the orphans thrown together in a pen not knowing where they are, but the most important thing of all is that they have no mothers. When a lamb has no mother it has no map; when the bond is broken between lambs and their mother they become a lost sheep.

I was once on a farm in Devon and was told about a hand-reared ewe called Judas. She lived in a slaughterhouse and when the lorries arrived crammed with nine-month-old lambs Judas would be placed at the bottom of the lorry ramp: her job was to lead the lambs into the slaughterhouse holding pen and she did this many hundreds of times throughout her life. The very handsome ram in the small paddock in front of the very cosy Burnt Pit Farm was being kept for a very different purpose, although it didn't look as if things were working out too well as he was in one corner of the paddock and a lone ewe was in the other.

As human beings we tend to look at a field of sheep or a skein of geese flying overhead and assume they are all the same. They are not – each ewe, each ram, each lamb, every goose, like us has its own individual character. Human beings have been very successful in depersonalising the natural world into lists of species, subspecies, genes, life cycles, holding pens, dairy units.

We reinforce this way of seeing by knowing one robin by the patterns of behaviour we observe in all robins, thus rendering them all similar. However, I love the way children, and girls especially, talk to animals. They address animals quite naturally as individuals, and I worry that it is the categorisation of the natural world by predominantly adult male scientists which has created an emotionally broken reflection of all other life forms, especially as the narrative of those who care for a horse, a dog, a cat or a lamb tells the story of just how transforming those individual relationships can be. It is our brethren in the natural world who really know us for what and who we are.

The horses had taken over the fields leading up to Dry Hill Farm. Row upon row of wooden-fenced blocks have replaced rows of apple and pear trees. These pony paddocks are really no more than politely fenced prisons; none of them I saw provided anything like in any way enough room for the horses to gallop, they are little better than cages. In the view to the north was childhood kingdom. From Dry Hill the distant trees were the colour of bracken and river water; they appeared soft, without edges, and small enough to harbour dens, and I knew where the snipe hid up in watery meadows, where the frogspawn coalesced behind the rushes, and which fields the orange-tip butterflies preferred. Rising up beyond the trees nine miles away was the giant dark green wave of the North Downs and above that an autumn blue sky. None of it seemed in focus and in the absolute stillness it was almost impossible to be sure any of it was real. Farms right on the brow of hills tend to have a much harder edge, mostly because they are comparatively unprotected on all sides, Dry Hill Farm is not nestled into the land as Burnt Pit Farm is. They do not share the same comforts; up here the work is harder because the wind is fiercer.

Just before the path rises southwards on to the whaleback summit and Dry Hill Fort there is a little clump of houses and a lovely shabby row of stables. In front of them stood a leafless apple tree festooned with dark red apples; it was a Christmas decoration more than anything else. Bryony and dog roses do the same – they also shed their leaves and these garlands of almost orange bryony berries are left strewn over hedges and draped from blackthorns with the rich red rose hips that hang alone to soften in the first frosts. There is a barely noticeable fort at all on the top of Dry Hill and not much more than a very lonely fence; archaeologists say the fort was never permanently occupied and have suggested it was built just in case it might be needed. What is much more impressive is the old beech tree that stands just beneath the brow of the hill in the centre of a plantation of much more recently established trees. Beech trees are monoecious – both male and female, producing flowers of both sexes. This one is carved with initials and a few hearts; within which male and female human beings have left their feelings for each other – etched into the tree which must have been at least 200 years old. Lovers have clearly been coming up here long before the trees that now surround it were planted. Perhaps, those who cut down all the other trees of a similar age spared it purposefully, consciously; that those doing the felling let it stand because of what was written into it.

Horses had churned the path into a buttery mud but it eased on the other side of the hill where the view opens out southwards over the tops of trees and into the distance of Ashdown Forest. Going into Jules Wood, I disturbed a pair of bullfinches; the male is such a dandy with a vivid pink red breast, blue lapels and a bright white rump when he takes to the air. Bullfinches have a penchant for the flower buds of fruit trees, making them extremely unpopular with fruit farmers, and up until 1996 it was legal to kill them. It is still legal to kill them – you just need to apply for a licence from Natural England: now there's a contradiction in terms. With each passing year I find it harder and harder to kill and the justification for doing so becomes more and more stringent. I now only kill to eat, and only then when the mackerel and the prawns are in, but slowly I am becoming vegetarian. I look back at the boy who shot sparkling starlings and stole robins' eggs and who killed and set butterflies not ten miles from here, knowing that each time he measured his strength through the sights of a gun he began to understand that each life he took made him weaker, not stronger. That to kill and set butterflies and then to hang them on the wall in boxes is not decoration, it is abomination, and that in doing so he learned that each instance of beauty is fleeting, that what is beautiful is ever changing, moving, ending and becoming, and slowly he began to understand that this is why he could never possess it. A silence had sunk beneath the canopy of trees in Jules Wood. Nothing stirred, the air remained where it was, and I became aware of how much noise I create just by walking.

In time the path emerges and swings round the edge of a field, where there is another wonderful view to the north before turning into the butterfly shaped Ten Acre Wood. It is not only our hearing that is enhanced by the stillness, the unmoving air holds the scent of things much more completely, and just before reaching Crippenden Manor the unmistakable mealy aroma of mushrooms hit my senses. It was so powerful I thought they must have been all around me but there was only a small flowering of about five or six of them emerging in clay-like shapes from the base of a rotting log about ten feet away from the path. Crippenden Manor oozed order, the cars parked outside were polished, the flower beds neat, even the dwarf willow weeping over the tiny pond could have been following instructions – but all of it was begging for music. A man was driving past on a miniature tractor towing a trailer half full of leaves with a wire rake splayed over the back, and I asked him whether I was on the right track, but he was clearly working and didn't seem inclined to pass the time of day and did little more than throw his hand in the direction of a gate at the edge of the house. It led into a slippery field where the path then cut through a section of Liveroxhill Wood.

I have never seen so many ponds in one place. The higher ponds were, without exception, invariably banked by uneven mounds of earth: these must have been some of the pits from which iron ore and clay were extracted in the sixteenth and seventeenth centuries. The lower ponds are hammer and furnace ponds. A hammer pond is formed by damming a stream. A waterwheel would have been placed just in front of the dam and to have provided muscle for the smelting bellows and large hammers which were used to force pig iron into refined bars. At its height the Weald produced 9,000 tons of iron a year, but the pits have turned into pools whose water is as black as moorhen feathers and the hammer ponds have mostly filled with silt and become tangled bogs giving life to tribes of flies.

The light from the lowering sun was coming in horizontally over a field on the brow of a small hill to the west of Liveroxhill Wood, which is probably why the small gathering of red deer hinds grazing in the next field didn't see me. The fox who was lounging in the grass in front of them didn't notice me either but he had his back to me. This would be a relaxing day for foxes and a hungry day as well; there would be very little food as his every movement would be heard. I love the way deer move: it is like watching the chorus of a ballet. They have innate grace and natural courtesy, it is as if they are continually dancing – and out in the open when they break as a herd they turn into a river. The first language of the natural world is body language, it is a rich vocabulary full of signals and subtleties, posture and gesture. A red deer signals alarm by quickly standing upright and raising its neck and tail. Having clearly caught sight of me – the decision was made within a couple of seconds and in one movement they broke for the woods. As they did so the fox turned, and saw me approaching and bolted, then melted away like a wanted man in a crowd; foxes are born with a guilty conscience.

On the other side of the field the path passes a line of four or five descending ponds and then sinks into a delightful hollow way. I have never smelt crab apples before I have seen them; I have picked them up and taken in that acidic sweet aroma but I have never stumbled upon it, but because the air was so still it held little pockets of exquisite scent as the apples lay where they fell around their dark-barked trees. It was heady and seductive, an exotic interruption amidst the altogether more erotic scent of fermenting mud and decaying leaves.

As the banks increased in height the path sank into shadow, below the reach of the sun with the light forming almost a roof of shafts above me. The last of the blazing sun always seems sharper in late November; there isn't the heat haze of summer in the air and so the light is still muscular and even. Because spring was so late this year a few of the trees, especially the smaller ones, have held onto just about all of their leaves; the hazels have turned tapioca, but the field maples look as if they are in bloom. Looking up through these trees frilling with lemon yellow leaves holding all that light against a background of fresh blue, to have seen it – to have taken it in – remains an aching beauty, a physical passion. As the path sank deeper between the banks on either side the last of the sun tangled up the branches above me with their own shadows. It had set by the time I reached the road, handing over the hedges and trees into the beginning of a quiet and breathing, thickening grey.

The minor road runs just above the stream that separates Kent from Sussex, passing soft-bricked houses and another hammer pond. The birds were sorting out the last of the issues of the day. Blackbirds in particular seem to have a good deal to say as the dusk sinks in, and a couple of males were squaring up to each other on the road in front of Smithers Farm where the path leads through an unusually tall gate into a copse. It continued along the floor of a valley, leading through copses and small, uneven fields where wisps of mist began to settle out of nowhere, before eventually rising above them on the approach to Upper Stonehurst Farm, where I held a couple of gates open for an elderly gentleman driving a tractor. Stretched out along the horizon was a band of brilliant red, really the colour of poppies, it was made all the more vivid set against the greying sky, but the grass was taking on dew and by the time I reached a stile leading into the field to take me back to the car I realised it was just about too dark to cross. Several lively looking bullocks were parked up against the fence. It is not a good idea to cross fields with cattle or horses in them at night.

On the map, a minor detour ran up past a barn and out on to a minor road, from where it was just a short hop back to the car – but there was a horse loose in the floodlit yard next to the barn. I watched by the gate for a while as four teenage girls tried to persuade him to walk sweetly into his night-time accommodation, a stable in the corner of the yard. They tried hay, which he just ate; they tried haylage, which he also ate, then they tried catching him, which he didn't seem at all partial to. At last, having caught him, they tried pulling him but he was a great deal stronger than they were and so he led them, mostly by the lead rein, round and round the top of the yard and back to the gate and as night fell the whole thing dissolved into a black-and-white comedy. The plot thickened when an idiot stepped in and offered to help.

I am not a rider of horses: I would rather my own legs did the walking. In Australia I mucked out a palomino stallion most mornings when I was working as a jackaroo and he taught me that the first thing a horse looks for in a human being is respect. I sidled up to the gate and we had a chat. I took the lead rein and stood beside him, ran my hand through his mane then took the bridle and started walking him down to the stable. He stopped halfway across the yard and that is where he stayed. We talked a little more. Horses have a wilderness in their eyes. I felt that he was fearlessly independent, that he loathed the coat he was wearing – he saw it as demeaning, he didn't care for being looked after at all, he knew he was a captive and I could be as persuasive and as charming as I liked but I was still the jailer. As I wandered back to the car I was left feeling that perhaps the time is fast approaching when we should set all the horses free.

Dry Hill, Sussex
Start and finish: OS map 147. Grid reference 414413
Time: three hours

▶ There are a good couple of parking spaces where the path begins on the minor road heading south-east out of Dormansland just beyond Ladycross Farm. The path is well marked from there and leads over a field.

▶ On the other side of the field turn left onto a metalled driveway, which becomes the Kent–Sussex border path at Old Lodge Farm. Continue along the metalled path to Dry Hill Farm and then, staying on the Kent–Sussex Border path, south-east up and over Dry Hill.

▶ Continue on the path, which will take you to Jules Wood. Here, the path almost doubles back on itself. You will find yourself in the middle of the wood, but continue onwards until the path emerges at the side of a field. The path down

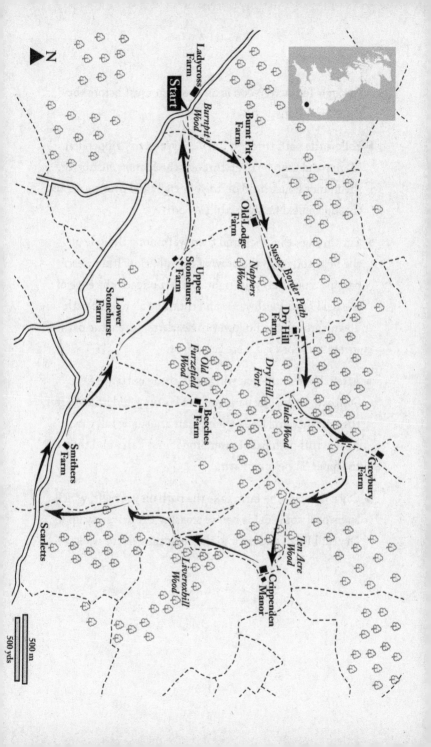

through Ten Acre Wood is on your right just before the wood runs out.

▶ Follow the path through Ten Acre Wood to Crippenden Manor and then head up through the Manor. Just before the manor house head off to your right and over a gate and through a field to Liveroxhill Wood.

▶ Cut through the wood and then walk along the side of the field and up to the brow of the hill. Here head west, passing a pond on your right. Once you reach the edge of the field head southwards and continue along this path down through the holloway to Scarletts, where the path meets a minor road: here turn right.

▶ After about a mile you will arrive at the entrance to Smithers Farm. The path you need is on your left just after the entrance and leads through an unusually tall gate. Follow this path past Lower Stonehurst Farm and then up to Upper Stonehurst Farm.

▶ Once through the farm take the path on your left, which leads over some fields before crossing the driveway up to Dry Hill Farm and back to the beginning of the walk.

Upper Ellastone, Staffordshire–Derbyshire border

Roots in stones

I have put two peacock butterflies in a drawer next to my bed. I found them on a windowsill, their bodies soft with life but overcome with the need to sleep. The drawer is slightly open so when the temperature and the rhythm of the light are right they will wake into a completely different world. December does not relent; time is tightened and the sunlight is a meagre ration. Outside the land is soaked in greys, all the bright colours have been packed away underground and the seeds locked up in a cold, wet earth.

The further north I drove, the heavier the grey became. In Upper Ellastone the only sign of bright colour was a basket of yellow tennis balls that had been placed next to the net on the court behind the village hall. This was a day when all the cars kept their lights on, and the dogs would get short walks; no one wears pink on days like these. Rising up behind the village hall are the Weaver Hills, they are the first indication that from here, going north, the land begins to change. That from here on in, the balance between arable and wild land begins to shift in earnest as the Pennines rise into the black moors of the Peak District then on into the Yorkshire Moors, the Lake District, the Northumberland hills, and beyond them the Lowlands of Scotland – hundreds of miles of mountains which still hide a few ptarmigan whose plumage will now be almost white. The forecast had said rain all day. None was falling as I set off underneath a roof of travelling clouds.

As the path turns off a small road between two houses I was greeted by a middle-aged couple who were unpacking their shopping. We said good morning. 'Are you going far then?' the man asked. I said that I was heading over to Stanton then down to Ordley Brook. 'It'll be a bit mucky down there. Have you got a jacket? Because the weatherman said it's pouring down all day.' In the field behind the house the ground was sodden with droplets of water glued, it seemed, on to almost every blade of grass, which in the hollows could barely absorb the underlying water.

Above me a lone lapwing danced in the air; they are forlorn alone. As a child I would watch huge flocks of them, thousands of birds or more out of a back seat window of my mother's car, but over the last thirty years their numbers have plummeted dramatically. At the root of this tragedy is not, in fact, the casual brutalities driven by the economics of intensive farming; it is the fact that we don't seem to be able to feel this loss. The few lapwings that do remain tend to hold out in the winter on the margins of flooded fields or where the land is not so well drained.

Everything became a little less slippery on the brow of the hill above Upper Ellastone. On the other side a bowl of a valley opens out into a puzzle of dry stone walls, a collection of loosely configured rectangles, oblongs and squares. On the slopes leading down to these dry stone walls are small stands of trees and the grassed-over hillocks of quarries and to the north, sandwiched between the fields and the sky, a slice of wild land the colour of a doormat and perched alongside it a small farm. But it was the Weaver Hills that I kept turning back to, looking at the darkening grass beneath the line of the ridge. It is a deep call, the call of the distance, which is heightened by its wild tones; the sea always beckons as well – or more, perhaps, what lies beyond it. We are hard wired to explore, to go into the distance and deep into the detail, to find new combinations of chords, new fusions of glass and space, to learn the language of another's lips. We are all thieves.

At the base of the valley is a syrup-coloured stream that steals under the grass. The small bridge was rickety and of course slippery and the path on the other side was now more of a bog than anything else. It led to a gate and then into a series of fields where the grass had been cropped low, to an even green. There are no wooden stiles over the dry stone walls, but there is a V-shaped gap where the path meets the wall. These are 'squeeze stiles'– human beings can get through them but sheep cannot. Some of these squeeze stiles are hundreds of years old and over that time human beings, especially in the West, have, shall we say, increased in height and girth.

I was talking to Gordon Wilton, who is a master in the craft of dry stone walling, and he was telling me that he was called out a couple of years ago because a generously proportioned woman had somehow become wedged into a squeeze stile, surely pure comedy gold. He said he was still building squeeze stiles along with 'lonky holes', which are rounded spaces in the walls for sheep to pass through from one field to another, and smaller openings at the base of walls called 'badger smoots', built to allow the animals to roam freely over the land.

The great spotted woodpecker that bounced through the air above me does not have to find any doorways. There is a male that comes and hangs off the bird feeder in front of my desk window; these birds are skittish and are grim reapers of house martin chicks breaking into their mud made nests. But it was a flash of almost tropical exuberance that pierced the heavy December sky. The fields here are small and precise, they felt old and left alone in this little valley. On my wall is a picture from 1944 of a view across the Downs from the Long Man of Wilmington over to Firle Beacon. What has changed in the last seventy years is that most of the hedges have gone: with the arrival of tractors and combines fields have trebled, quadrupled, in size. The rule of thumb used to be that a field was the area big enough for one man to work alone.

The small barn on the brow of the hill before Stanton sat beautifully within this landscape. The walls must be a foot thick. It didn't appear to be used at all; the sheep had been in but I reckon it will still be there 500 years from now. The view from the entrance wanders south and on a clear day must extend for twenty miles but the distance was shrouded in a vapour that undid every outline. I clambered down a steep bank into a smaller valley where water was running over the grass at the bottom and then up an equally steep bank into Stanton, which sits into the side of a hill. The streets were empty, there was no one about. The only sign of life was the noticeboard tacked on to the side of what had obviously been a barn, but there didn't seem to be a lot going on behind the glass. I kept looking up at the sky. It was bruised but it didn't feel as if it was going to rain; there was even a little warmth in the light wind.

Turning out of Stanton, the path crosses a field, then over a muddy little brook and follows a line between Smithy Moor Farm and Eldergreave Cottage, but somewhere between the two it simply vanishes. So having jumped a ditch I wandered towards the corner of the field and entered the top of a steep-sided wooded valley – the path leading down is a delight. The wind wasn't strong enough to be heard but it was clearly there, because occasionally the trees would creak and growl. On the ground there are ferns but there were no footprints.

On the map this arm of the wood is marked by the words 'Motcarn Sprink'. Halfway down the path before it reaches the valley floor is a forty-foot rock face out of which grows a rugged old oak. I have only seen trees growing directly out of rock in the white stone mountains above the Shaolin Temple in China; they also cling to the sides of the gorges in south-western Crete. It is a relationship that seemingly defies convention. These trees are always fascinating – because they exist beyond the rigorous grip of 'normal': and in them lies the possibility of enchantment and there the invitation to know ourselves in a completely different mirror.

There is something so primal about a rock face; most of us quite naturally walk up and touch it, we run our hands over it. On the walls of the newly discovered Chauvet Cave in the Ardèche in southern France are mesmeric pictures of rhino, lions and wild horses, the earliest of these images is 32,000 years old. *Homo sapiens* has spent more time living in caves than in anything else; we carry that history in our cells. I have always found the paths that run along the base of rock faces to be incredibly comforting places; I already know them as places that offer the potential of safety and protection, and that is the way I see Motcarn Sprink, this curiously named and beautiful forty-foot rock face in the middle of a wood in the middle of England.

Flowing along the valley is Ordley Brook, a slow brown stream running under branches with deeper pools carved into some of its corners and patches of yellow white foam blanketing some of the surface. Lying across the path that quietly follows the stream as it heads down through the wood are several fallen trees. I liked the way they had just been left there and how in places people had walked round them and in others clambered over them, and the one plank bridge that cuts over the water, it sat perfectly in the midst of the wood. It is surely an art to be able to create and place stiles and bridges in a manner that complements the land they inhabit. The path running through this wood feels as if it has been formed over generations, it does not link one hamlet, one village, to another, it has simply evolved over time as human beings chose to walk this way simply because the way is nothing other than beautiful. It is a pleasure to be here; the path has no practical purpose. Paths that have evolved just to give pleasure and solace, space – and these are often incidental paths running through woods or leading up to waterfalls or curving along the ledges under rock faces – are just as much a part of our history as the practical path joining one farm to another or a church to a village. These are the paths that lovers walk and these are the places that we come to wrestle with forgiveness, to grieve alone, to untie knots and be refreshed and renewed by beauty.

Just before the path emerged from the wood where the valley widens into a scrubby little field I heard the call of a coal tit, its evenly repeated notes. I haven't seen one for a while; they are not as numerous as the blue and great tits. Coal tits look as if they are a combination of a blackcap and a blue tit, but what sets them apart from other titmice, which is their country name, is that they stash food in hidden larders in their territories; they are hoarders.

There must have been a building of some kind, maybe an old cart shed at the edge of the wood. What remains is a distinct line of stones all of them covered, almost wrapped up in a soft bright green moss, it was a burst of primary colour amidst hundreds of different shades of brown and grey. Beyond the scrubby field the path joins a minor road and then heads downwards across another single-plank bridge over the stream before climbing up what is quite a steep rise to The Hutts Farm. In the paddock beyond the farm were two horses who came up and said hello and it was then I realised that, apart from a few distant sheep grazing on the Weaver

Hills, all the fields had been empty, there had been no sheep or cattle in any of them.

I was back in the land of hedgerows. The dry stone walls had gone, and on this side of Ordley Brook there are definitely more trees, and running along the top of the hill to the south was a ploughed field where a few pheasants were scratching for food. I crossed back over the brook into the field beneath Northwood Farm. It stretches out along the valley floor giving way to the woods at the far end; and somewhere down there is surely a sweetly grassed bank sloping down to the edge of the water. In several places in the wood the brook had thrown up these little yellow sand beaches. These fresh-water beaches are wonderful places to lie up in the summer, to strip off and swim and feel the current on your skin.

Northwood Farm feels like more of a hamlet: low barns and a collection of stocky little houses, but not much mud. The path leading back into Upper Ellastone meanders gently down over a field and heads directly for the church. It is an old practical path: children would have walked this way to school and men wobbled back from the pub, this path carried eggs and coffins, letters and washing. A band of very scraggy looking hens were hanging around by the church wall and there was a dead field mouse lying in front of the gate that leads into the churchyard. The mouse didn't seem to have been caught, it was perfect, there wasn't a mark on it – no tell-tale signs of having danced for a cat. Hens are unforgiving when it comes to order and food; I have seen them eat frogs, slow-worms and a young grass snake but they don't seem to eat mice.

The church porch was decorated for Christmas, bunches and sprigs of holly and ivy intermingled with gold flashing tinsel and a few glitter-covered pine cones that lay along the benches which sat either side of a big wooden door. I turned the handle but the door was locked. My heart sank. There are only a few things more broken than a locked-up church. The law of sanctuary was actually abolished in 1632, but up until then certain churches were by law compelled to provide sanctuary for anyone who felt they needed it. Usually those who fled into churches were being pursued by a lynch mob; our modern laws of asylum have their roots in the medieval laws of sanctuary.

Winter carries a knife. We don't feel it that often. I am protected to a certain degree by central heating, hot water and layers of clothing that have been technically designed to keep me warm but really winter in these lovely islands is nothing other than hostile. A couple of years ago I was having a conversation with a regular in the pub in my home village. He told me that he was driving home one winter's evening across the park, the mist was floating in sheets and as he neared his house two young children, a boy and a girl, walked across the lane, passing through the beam of the car headlights. What struck him and his wife who sat beside him was that the children were dressed in Victorian clothing. They were ghosts.

Some time in the 1850s there was a family living in Beddingham, which is two miles from where the children were seen. The mother of the children died and the father began to exact a reign of terror over the household; he apparently beat the children. No one knows what happened that night, but whatever it was led to these two young children leaving the house long after dark to walk over the fields to their grandmother's house. Their bodies were found in the morning, huddled together in a hedge. They had frozen to death.

In these islands, winter is hard because it is physically testing. Our story of winter is one told by gritters and flu, sales and television, and in the almost apologetic expressions of weather forecasters. If I am to believe them I will miss winter's greatest gift; be unable to see its maverick beauty. In winter I am living in a strange land. The trees have turned black and thunderous, there are no flowers. Rooks and crows have captured the sky and just under half the population of birds have left, they have flown south, the butterflies sleep, and apart from the rain and wind the land is quiet, so quiet. The great gift of winter is the gift of rest.

— ✺ —

Upper Ellastone, Staffordshire – Derbyshire border

Start and finish: OS map 259. Grid reference 435116
Time: three hours

....

▶ I parked in the village hall car park and from here turned left out of the car park and headed uphill. About 300 yards further on there is a path on your right that leads between two houses: take it. This leads on to the brow of a hill then down into the valley and over the stream.

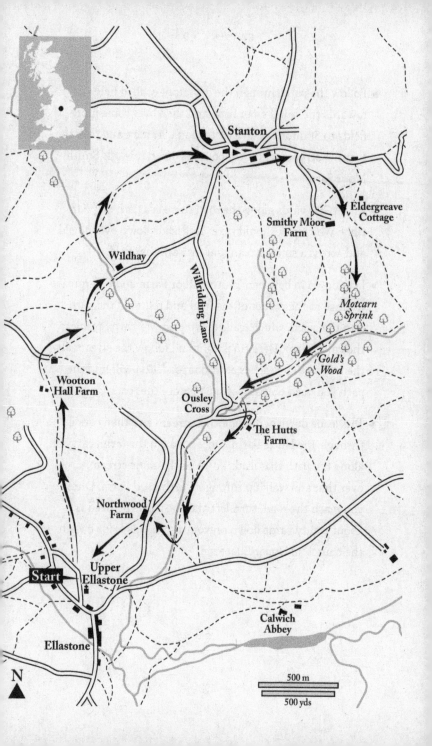

▶ Follow the path through the dry-stone-walled fields up towards the small stout barn and then over some more fields to Stanton. Head east through Stanton and take the turning on your right, which leads down towards Smithy Moor Farm.

▶ About 200 yards along the road there is a path on your right, which you should take. This leads down over a field and across a small stream out into another field.

▶ I cut down in between Smithy Moor Farm and Eldergreave Cottage to the corner of the field and followed the path into the wood, which leads down past Motcarn Sprink to the valley floor. Here turn right and follow the stream all the way until it reaches a tarmac road. You will find the path you need on your left just before the road.

▶ This leads down across another stream and then cuts up through The Hutts Farm. Once through the farm, carry on along the path that leads down to the same stream. Cross over that and walk up through Northwood Farm. Once you reach the road, turn left and the path you need is about eighty yards down on your right. This leads back to the church in Upper Ellastone.

The Hoo Peninsula, Kent

Everyone's gone to the moon

The Isle of Grain on the Hoo Peninsula is a place in between the land and the sea. Delta land, with the Thames on one side and the River Medway on the other, it has been pushed into existence by silt. From the silt came the salt marsh, the sea coming and going creeping inwards, sliding up channels of mud, hiding crabs that on summer nights would occasionally venture up into the grass of a few small, scattered dry islands. The Romans were the first to attempt to drain the marshland to create the pasture which now exists at high tide below the level of the sea; it is a land enclosed by banks of earth and when the winter rains arrive it turns into a wetland and comes alive with ribbons of birds.

It had been raining on and off for over a week, with one Atlantic storm following another; even the Christmas lights hanging off the gutters and draped down the porches of some of the houses in Allhallows were unable to dispel the sense of melancholia. There are very few places further away from home than the cul-de-sacs of modern houses in the backlands of villages enduring a pewter December sky. Occasionally there would be a flurry of wind and handfuls of rain but it wasn't constant, this swirl would last for just a minute or so, moving plastic dustbins, and spinning crows, which they seemed to be enjoying.

The path leads down on to the marsh from the back of Allhallows. Looming over the marshland to the east is the second-tallest chimney in the UK. Standing at 801 feet, it was part of a coal-fired power station that was converted to oil but has been mothballed since 2012. Next to the old power station is a new one that burns natural gas and provides electricity for over a million homes, and next to that stand the round, cream-coloured storage tanks of an oil refinery. To the right of them are the skeletons of several massive cranes. I would imagine the whole area is fenced: these facilities are the engine room of our society, but they have been placed on the edges, they are far enough away for us not to feel the swell of their shadows.

Something had disturbed the cattle. There was a long line of them charging along the sea bank in the distance; it looked as if it might be the beginning of an organised attempt to commandeer a vessel to take them to Devon. The fields carved out of the marsh were either underwater or so sodden that every footstep I took on the grass left its impression in mud; this is just how the gulls and wading birds love it.

I could see Terry from some way off, a man alone in the

land, and as I came closer it became clear that he was standing on the path behind a tripod as tall as he was. We said good morning and then he looked down at my boots. 'Where you heading for?' he asked. I explained that I was taking the path to the sea bank then following it round to Allhallows on sea. 'Well, you should be all right. There's a very boggy bit just beyond the stile and then the rest of it isn't much better but just before the sea bank it is truly atrocious, the cattle have really mucked it up.'

I asked him what birds were on the wetland and he explained that there were herring gulls, black-headed gulls and a few lapwing. ' There were seventeen marsh harriers,' he said, 'but several of them have skipped off to Sheppey so I think there are only about thirteen left here now.' He was dressed in bird-watching gear, which tends to be thicker, more robust than and not quite as all-enclosing as the clothes the still fishermen wear as they sit six feet in front of the waves in January and February waiting for their lines to tighten. I asked whether many people walked this way and he said there were a few more in the summer and that the locals were trying to open a footpath around the industrial area next to the village of Grain but the scheme was being blocked by one landowner. Now, in the winter, there are only twitchers and dog walkers. We said goodbye and as I was walking away he shouted, 'Here comes a harrier – it's a male,' and I turned to see this brown bomber of a bird gliding low and evenly over the wetlands.

Terry was right about the path. There were no human footprints, just huge great hoof holes filled with rain in ponds of grey mud which it became increasingly difficult to find a way round. The wide ditches on either side of the path just in front of the sea bank were full to the brim with black water and swaying stands of sedge: the path was more a river of clay, shit and water. It would not have been possible or safe for a child to cross it. Some kind or desperate soul had lobbed a few bricks into this mix. They were about a yard apart. I stood on the first one and immediately it sank into the mire so I jumped for the next: it held firm. But halfway across there were no more, or they had simply been swallowed up.

Every year a handful of walkers have to be rescued because they have become stuck in mud; usually this happens on mudflats. Some time ago I was invited by a seasoned Fenlander to walk out at low tide into the Wash to meet the seals. He took with him a long length of rope, which he said he hoped we wouldn't need. He must have been in his late sixties or early seventies, yet when we reached the mudflats he handed me the rope, grinned, then started running. That's how we did it, taking it in turns to run across the mud-filled channels. So there was only one thing to do.

Across the tea-coloured estuary water to the north, Southend seemed to be in various stages of decay – just a collection of blocks that came and went depending on the consistency of the drizzle, which did the same. Up on the top of the sea bank the path was only a little better than the one that led over the fields. It seemed the tide was coming in, lapping at the graduated concrete squares that had been laid to protect the bank from the salt water. For a while it rained, and then cleared again just before I reached a small cockle bank: although it was made entirely of shells it was the colour of new sand. Lying among the broken pieces of whelks and the occasional blue flash of mussel shells were a few little Baltic tellins. These are robust and small almost heart-shaped shells that arrive on the shoreline of estuaries and mudflats, they have clearly distinct semi-oval growth rings. I have seen them in orange, in white and yellow, but they also come in green, which I have never found. These were a dog-rose pink.

The oldest items of jewellery worn by human beings have been carbon-dated as around 100,000 years old: they are shells and they were found in a cave in Israel. Were they picked up and threaded onto plaited grass, were they incidental or were they important? Were they given or were they taken, were they purely decorative or did they carry a symbolic meaning for the human being who was wearing them? Nowadays they still do. Those who wear gold chains around their necks are telling you they are chained to gold. Those who wear a single shell are saying something completely different.

The sea bank curves slowly into Allhallows-on-Sea, where it runs around the edge of a holiday chalet park, a loosely configured collection of large brown sheds and occasional patches of stacked white plastic chairs; when I was there, it was completely empty. Beyond the chalets is a static caravan site and in front of that a beach no bigger than a few canoes. Most of the caravan windows displayed similar notices: 'All valuable items have been removed from this caravan.' By that they surely mean televisions, laptops, watches, microwaves, and most definitely gold jewellery – but a comfortable bed is surely worth a great deal to a weary man.

I was beginning to tire of concrete – it was everywhere: the sea wall, the path, even the benches – and then I came across a garden. It was placed under the front of one of the caravans. It was a fairyland of small concrete animals, squirrels, moles and, mice; I think there was a fawn there as well. They were standing among heathers and polyanthus, forming an aria, a shrine set in the middle of antiseptic order, which made it all the more beautiful. At the end of the caravan park is Allhallows Yacht Club, completely encased in wire mesh fencing topped with several strands of barbed wire; mercifully it looked as if everyone had managed to escape. The whole place reeked of the presence of thieves.

Beyond Allhallows-on-Sea, the marsh smelt of dogs and oil, the path petered out and it was unclear whether I should stick to a small bank which had a couple of poles stuck in it, or whether – along with pieces of pallets, the odd rotting trainer, half-eaten footballs and enough plastic to build a boat with – the poles were just part of the mix I should head for. The small strand of beach seemed a better option and there was the reassuring presence of a clear set of footprints; however, they mysteriously vanished almost as soon as they started. Barely a stone's throw further on, the beach became impassable when it reached a large creek; beyond it stood a half-submerged pillbox and a gathering of oystercatchers and sandpipers, which swarmed into the air forming one beating heart, falling, folding and rising into sails and waves. The purpose of this exquisite dance is to mesmerise the peregrine falcons, to utterly confuse their focus.

Gingerly I cut back through a carpet of sea purslane and jumped a couple of small creeks, making my way towards the fence and the fields, not seeing that the widest of the ditches lay just in front of the sea bank. It was full of black timbers, the bones of a long-abandoned boat that had fallen to pieces over time, as the highest of tide came and rearranged the litter and gently pulled the deck from the hull, dismantling the carcass bit by bit until its original form was rendered unimaginable. This is part of the work of storms, part of the work of winter and the wind – to destroy, to clear all that went before, to create a clean space for new life, new shapes and new melodies of colours.

A kind soul had placed one of the timbers from the broken boat over the creek; it was thin and slippery, but it worked. I loved the land just behind the marsh, it was more of a flat wide drove with various pools and the odd leafless hawthorn tree, a place for voles and grass snakes and a wide enough hunting ground for barn owls and a pair of kestrels that took off, heading for some large sycamores standing at the end of the field. Hawthorn trees often stand alone in the wildest of places; I have seen single trees in the middle of miles of moor and growing alone on the sides of mountains. They are both robust and delicate, and they are heavy with folklore symbolising fertility and purity, but more than that they broker enchantment, undoing reality, decorum and balance. Hawthorn trees flower in May but each tree has a slightly different coloured blossom, running through the spectrum from pure white extending in various shades to a deep red. It is the sight, and the also the scent, of these trees flowering in May that has commandeered the whole month to be named after it: May blossom smells thick and oily, a combination of almonds and petrol, and many country people still consider it unlucky to bring these flowers into the home because their scent is not that dissimilar to that of the dead.

Moving upriver, the breathing flow of the Thames narrows and the marsh gives out into flat fields which extend northwards, holding a few lonely trees and a scattering of grey sheep grazing behind mended fences. The path then enters a small copse where it becomes a flowing stream, the water draining off the even hill that leads down to the marsh from the south. It was too deep to walk and it was difficult finding a way through the closely planted young trees on either side of it. Perched on top of the hill sits a very bereft and austere-looking farmhouse. Nothing on the Isle of Grain feels isolated but the farmhouse somehow lacked any kind of tenderness; it was as if no one had laughed out loud there for a long time. The bulrushes in one of the larger pools spoke a very different language. Some were rupturing their seeds, turning their sleek brown heads into an ochre down. Each bulrush head produces around 220,000 seeds and the plants are a wild superfood. The young shoots can be eaten either raw or stir-fried and are delicious. Pancakes can be made from the pollen of the flowers and the root tubers contain ten times more starch than potatoes, but also a great deal more gluten than wheat.

There is another long narrow field that heads south and up towards Coombe House the grass here was wet and heavy. I could see the sky darkening in the west, promising another bucket of rain. Rather than following the road the path runs through a small spinney opposite Coombe House – or at least I thought it did. I was doubling back when a young man with curly brown hair appeared in the driveway of the house. He smiled and wished me a Happy New Year and looked up at the sky and asked me how far I was going. I reckoned it was a couple more miles.

More than any other season, winter takes you into a solitary room and, if I am brave enough to follow it, to the empty lands of desolation; it is the most profoundly alien of all the seasons, the most unknown and the least visited. Our natural reaction to winter is usually to try and brighten it up with tinsel and talk of spring, but the older I become, the more inclined I am to let it work its deep emotional magic of clearing and resolving. Winter is the healer of the deepest wounds. So when the young man asked me how far I was going, I really had no idea; I was in the solitary room far away from tinsel and all talk of spring.

From Coombe House the path almost doubles back, running just beneath the brow of the hill leading down to the Thames estuary and wanders right up against the brick wall that stands in front of the austere farmhouse. What I hadn't noticed from the marsh was a barn, and, like many barns, it was full of things we think we might one day need, things we have put aside. Garages and lofts are the same: more than anything they contain a material history of our lives. Someone had stacked a long line of bricks up against the farmhouse wall so I sat for a while and watched Southend veer in and out of focus and the small monotone dots of oystercatchers flying almost in formation low over the brown water. Large droplets of rain started to fall as I walked down Homewards Road, which on the map seems to be completely without a purpose: it is simply three sides of a square and has no destination, a piece from one puzzle in the box of another. The finishing touch was a speed camera road sign that must have been removed from its stand on some A road and attached to the back of a sign that I should have looked at the front of, but the rain was truly falling by then.

The last section of the walk runs down to the fence at the back of the caravan park before cutting across the centre of a large field and back to Allhallows. Lying on the path was a small red oblong piece of plastic. Written on it were the words 'The Doghouse', with a web address and a strapline which read 'Positive training'. It was the only bright colour I had seen on this beautifully desolate day in all the wet running paint of these tidal lands.

I can't remember exactly when, but once I saw a painting of a single marker pole out at sea – that was all it was, and I wish I knew the name of the artist. It remains a profoundly powerful statement about the reach and the isolation of human existence. This little red piece of plastic spoke for the painting, a creation that seemed completely out of place, marooned in the very world that created it. To be alone in a landscape like this one leads inexorably into the depths and mysteries of communion. In the next few thousand years we will undoubtedly discover that the universe is ebbing and flowing with life and that we have never been just endlessly drifting.

Allhallows, the Isle of Grain, Kent

Start and finish: OS map 163. Grid reference 775835
Time: four hours

▶ I parked near the church and followed Binney Road, which
leads down past the church and some modern housing.
The path you need is on your right, just as the road bears
round to the left at the bottom of the village.

▶ This path takes you out on to the marshes and up on to
the sea wall: in winter you will need some good boots.
Once you reach the sea wall turn left and follow it all the
way into Allhallows-on-Sea.

▶ Continue through Allhallows-on-Sea and take the path
that begins on the other side of the Yacht Club. I got a bit
confused here, but I think the path runs over the marsh
to a very rickety bridge. You can either take that route or
wander along the small beach and cut up inland when you
hit the large creek.

▶ Once through the marsh, continue heading westwards
until you are just about underneath the whitewashed
Coombe House. Here head up the narrow field that leads
to the front of the house and then take the bridleway,
which almost doubles back on itself.

▶ Carry on for about a mile until you reach a minor road on
your right. Then head a short way along this minor road

N

500 m
500 yds

River Thames

Allhallows Marshes

Groynes

Kingsmead Park

Caravan Park

Allhallows

Groynes

Binney Rd.

Allhallows-on-Sea

Slipways

Groynes

Start

The Chimneys

Groynes

Ro:wards

Howards Road

Lower Stoke

Dagnam Saltings

Dagnam Farm

Newhall Farm

Brickhouse Farm

Noreland Cottage

Coombe House

and take the path that heads over the fields on your left, walking past Dagnam Farm.

► Stay on this path until you come to Homewards Road, which you follow until you come to an obvious corner: here take the path that is on the corner. This leads back to Allhallows-on-Sea and from here take the path over the fields back to Allhallows.

Trevigro, Cornwall

Winter's spring

Route 38 is an American diner that sits on a roundabout ten miles beyond Plymouth on the A38. As I walked in, Jim Morrison was coming through the speakers singing 'the future's uncertain and the end is always near'. On the walls above rows of red and blue bench seats hung chrome-framed pictures of Buddy Holly, the Beatles and Jon Bon Jovi. Beyond the windows the land was lit for the first time in many days and the fields were covered in an icing of frost, the white crystals sugaring the green. As the rising sun hit the hedges it illuminated the apparently dull bark into yellows, greens and wild reds: the world looked as if it was in the process of being made.

From the diner, I headed north towards Trevigro out on to narrower and narrower high-banked back roads and into a succession of wooded valleys, crossing over one-lane bridges and fords on the edge of woods. Most were streams but there was one river; I had to stop and take it in as the sun came cutting through the trees lining the banks, lighting up flecks of breath exhaled by the silver grey water. It was flowing fast; rising and rippling, it moved as a separate entity, writhing through the land, returning the storms to the sea. On the map there are not many footpaths running through inland Cornwall and in some places there is just an apparently random section of path which joins nothing, it starts on the other side of a field and it finishes next to a wood; maybe they are remnants, it is impossible to tell or perhaps there was no greater need for them in Cornwall – maybe freedom of movement was simply assumed. So some of this walk takes place on minor roads, which of course were once bridleways.

A cockerel was still crowing the morning in as I stepped out of the car in the small hamlet of Trevigro. Cockerels are more subdued on duller days. The sun didn't look as though it was going to last for long: a huge white bank of cloud haunted the edge of the western horizon. At this time of year the land is hungry for sunlight and when it arrives it comes as a flood, as food in a famine. It's on these blue winter days – with their copper sulphate skies, the sunlight breaking into the secrets that are being kept behind barks, melting rooms and burning shadows – that we can see how beautiful the elderly really are.

Most of the villages in this part of Cornwall seem to be sheltered into the sides of hills, in the folds nestling between west and east. This makes sense because the prevailing wind tends to come tearing in off the Atlantic and whilst the deeper valleys would provide more protection, they also have a lot less hours of sunlight. I headed east along a minor road up onto the brow of a small hill facing south over a collection of wooded valleys with various church spires puncturing a thin mist. Cornwall is really lit by the sea, the light bouncing off the water on three sides; it has, I think, the most beautiful daylight in the world. Yes, the very early mornings in the Sinai and Namibian deserts are scored in gold, and the way the sunshine is almost solid down at the bottom of the fabulous Cretian Gorges is unforgettable, but the Cornish light is a combination of sunlight and sea light stirred into the remnants of the moist tropical air which is delivered from the Atlantic Ocean.

As I walked down off the brow of the hill the road steepened, entering a wood where diamonds of ice fell from the trees. Droplets of water on the twigs had frozen in the night but were now beginning to thaw and fall. Leaving the road at the bottom of the valley, the path strolls up alongside what was a large swollen stream passing a tiny forgotten orchard; there were perhaps no more than nine or ten trees locked into a square piece of ground. They might have seemed out of place, but every branch, every twig was covered in grey-green lichen, hanging off every available surface in feathers and rags; the trees seemed marooned in the remains of a dream. A couple of hundred yards further on, the trunk of a much larger tree was growing horizontally over the ground, lying there encased in a rich green moss.

Even in the midst of winter these woods are sweet with ferns and fat with thriving mosses; there is movement, activity – these are not the sleeping woods of south-east England. There are reckoned to be about a thousand native mosses living on the beautiful islands of Great Britain, and they have some wonderfully evocative names: frigid grimmea, fallacious beard-moss and blushing bog-moss, to name just a few. It is also a possibility that even now, as they continue so sadly to decline, not all mosses may yet have been discovered.

Finding the path beyond the wood was impossible; there are no yellow waymarkers to be seen as the trees give out into bright fields. I decided the best thing to do was to head off in a vaguely north-easterly direction. This led to the end of a long field with no gate, so I plunged into the hedge and clambered over what was left of a dry stone wall in the middle of it, then under barbed wire on the other side. At first I couldn't hear the road, but it was there beyond a gate at the top of the field, an empty grey river hemmed in by hedges. Very occasionally a car would scoot past, but they all slowed down and every driver waved. Once they had passed the road was silent, although around it the birds sang ceaselessly, every note rising from every wood and tree rooting into the still air. It could have been half past four in the morning in May.

The village of Maders smelt of slurry, a pungent mixture of shit and sugar: the source was the black and white Friesian cows that were moping around and steaming in a sunlit barn to the side of the road. What came as a surprise was a field of ewes and lambs just beyond Maders. I stopped and leaned on the gate for a while and watched a small group of the slightly older lambs gambolling, running and skipping at the top of the field, their mothers calling them over when they saw me at the gate. Young animals and birds play. I know the behavioural biologists will tell us this is all about learning the lines of posture, testing strength and speed and laying down the first claims on place and status, but more than anything it speaks of unencumbered joy. Fully grown sheep are so serious, they graze apart from each other, they tend to sit separately in the fields and, rather than bunching together in the rain, they stand there alone, forlorn and motionless, completely self-contained. Lambs on the other hand are gregarious, mischievous and social; maybe it is because they have not been informed yet about the eating habits of wolves and man.

Bobbing and squabbling behind the ewes and lambs were eleven magpies – eleven for health, twelve for wealth and thirteen for the devil himself. Magpies trail a rich folklore in which they are more often than not cast as thieves. What I love about magpies is that they seem utterly impervious to all forms of disapproval. It is still legal to shoot and trap them on the grounds that they take the eggs and young of field and songbirds. But I have never seen them being mobbed by other birds. If there is a predator around such as a tawny owl or a sparrow hawk, the smaller birds gang together and move *en masse* as close as they dare, shouting and scolding; it's a fabulous racket. All the forces arraigned against magpies have not clipped their swashbuckling stance: they remain loud, iridescent, unbowed and – come what may – they continue to party.

Even in the sunlight, the lapwings standing around in a field further down the road seemed a great deal more subdued. A group of lapwings is called a 'deceit' and it used to be believed that lapwings inherited the souls of those who died in a troubled state; those who had been unable to forgive or had been embittered by the experience of love. There is no more saddening spell. The lapwings must have seen me as they hurried off the ground and circled several times above what was a very rare ploughed field, floating together in silence, tempting the fates of foreboding.

The sight of five pink campion flowers stopped me in my tracks. In just fourteen weeks' time the flowers of this year's bloom will be beginning to break from the buds – but here they were halfway up the bank on the side of the road drinking sunlight and soliciting bees. I rarely see the pink of their flowers anywhere else.

It is quite a steep climb up the road to South Hill, where there was another locked church and a parliament of rooks attempting to sort out who should nest where. This horse trading goes on in the canopies of trees throughout January, and it is not something that is done quietly. The road was silent; not one car drove past me between South Hill and Linkinhorne. In winter the roads are without doubt easier walking; there isn't the mud if it's cold and crisp, or as much referring to the map to contend with, and there are no doubts about the right direction to take. The downside is that it is harder to change your mind, to be seduced into climbing down the bank or lying up for a while next to a forgotten pond on the edge of a wood, watching for fish rising up from the depths to graze the surface of another world.

The grey granite tower of Linkinhorne Church is straight out of science fiction: I think it is six storeys high, if the turrets are included. The stone must have been quarried out of Bodmin Moor, which rises behind the tower. In the distance to the north are three peaks, Stowe's Pound, Stowe's Hill and the Cheese Ring; they were pinkish rounded casts of rocks concertinaed on top of each other.

Out of the three large moors in the south-west, Bodmin Moor is the most alone. Most people just drive through it on their way to the Cornish coast. It is smaller than Dartmoor and Exmoor and much less talked about, except perhaps as the location of Daphne du Maurier's Jamaica Inn. I first went there as a teenager. I was down at Constantine Bay, camping in a field with three friends, and we met some girls in the Farmers Arms in St Merryn. It was a surfers' pub then with a jukebox, slate floors and poky little outside loo. The girls invited us to a party in a house out on Bodmin Moor, and there we drank, we smoked, we danced, we kissed. She had this wild curly blonde hair and smelt of apricots and heather, we were seventeen, and her father picked her up just after midnight. Those of us who were left eventually crashed out in a heap in an upstairs room just as it was getting light. I didn't sleep much and a couple of hours later I wandered out on to the moor and lay down in the summer grass next to a whisky-coloured lake, listening to mallards and flies.

The owner of the house was the Cornish explorer Robin Hanbury-Tenison. I remember talking to him in the kitchen when I returned from the lake. I said how much I would like to travel, to know the tribal peoples of the rainforests and faraway islands. He explained that the process was fraught with difficulty because of influenza and many of the colds and coughs we have to deal with on a yearly basis; if the uncontacted peoples of the rainforest were to catch them they would more than likely die. It was a shocking revelation and I have never forgotten it; it said to me that wherever we go we carry with us a great deal more than a day pack and a walking stick – that it is the constantly evolving bacteria and viruses that are the givers of life and death in this world.

I never knew buzzards had lemon-yellow talons. This one must have been dead for at least a couple of weeks: it was lying cruciform on its stomach under a blackthorn tree with both wings spread on the top of the moss-covered dry stone wall down at the end of a field beneath Linkinhorne Church. It looked as if it had surrendered: all life ends in surrender. I think it was a young bird and it was surprising the foxes hadn't taken it; with all the rain perhaps they simply couldn't smell it. I was in the wrong field so I shambled through a small tangled copse alarmed with nettles in the corner, then over a tiny wooden bridge, the planks had turned green and were as slippery as ice.

On the other side the land rises again. The sheep in the field ran themselves together and stared intently as I once again tried to find a stile over the next wall. It was a diagonal set of stone steps that had been built into the wall and there were some which led me down. Looking south beyond the few houses of Mornick, I saw there was not one ploughed field, just a gathering of almost evenly spaced rounded hills all of them hemmed with woods. There is a noticeable absence of tractor tracks on the land and no signs shouting 'Keep Out' or 'Private Property'. Maybe it is simply the reality of topography and rain that has kept the blight of industrial arable farming at bay, for here the natural world is thriving – it hasn't been defeated. The land doesn't feel as if it is in a perpetual state of mourning; it is still joyous and it seeps into you. This natural joy is present throughout the world. I have felt it on a quiet path leading through the rainforest in Brazil, in the deserts of Egypt and Africa and in the early dusk of an Arctic afternoon in the stunted willow forests of northern Norway. It is not the windowless room of infatuation or the infertile flowers of sentimentality, it is the joy that prevails over the casual brutalities and the destructive fires of existence. This is the hymn the earth sings.

From Mornick the path heads south in various pieces to Trewoodloe. The stream at the bottom of another valley just before Lansugle Farm must have recently been a river and although most of the bridge had been swept away, a large section of it was left leaning into the water on the opposite bank. I should have taken my boots off and felt the cold current on my skin, but it was just a skip and a jump and one sock remained dry.

In Trewoodloe, a middle-aged man advised me that the cattle in the field leading down to Berrio were a little lively and had ambushed him and his dog yesterday morning, and that they tended to lurk just beyond the steep descent to the road. They must have been moved or were grazing in a further part of the field, so thankfully there was no need for bravado on both our parts.

Again the path was impossible to discern so I ended up walking through someone's back garden and then skinning the fence above the steep bank that dropped down to the road and the valley floor. I love walking beside rivers and the River Lynher was in full spate, this grey-blue water neatly slicing through the winding lines of trees. The water must have been right up over the banks no more than twenty-four hours ago: all the field grass had been flattened in the direction of the flow, and there were huge lumps of turf tangled into the branches dangling over the water and untidy compressed clusters of roots and twigs were crammed into various corners. Some rivers are really at their best in winter, nudging along between bright frosted fields or charging through a tunnel of leafless trees in a January wood. I wish I could have seen the weir that stands in the field before Bicton Mill but the path gave out and ran back to a road. This is a sweet valley; there is a gentleness here, nothing feels hurried. Watermills can only work at the speed of a river.

The sun started stuttering as I climbed a steep and rutted road that led up to the path back to Trevigro. This is a land I thought I knew. For the last fifty-odd years this is where I have found summer, as a boy rock-pooling and trawling the coves beyond Trevone for cowries. As a teenager lying around in the dunes that back on to Constantine Bay waiting for that dramatic rhythmic increase in volume as the big waves come in, and at night stumbling back the worse for wear in the early hours along the unlit road that leads from St Merryn to the sea. Apart from one venture out into the depths of Bodmin Moor, the Cornwall I have known has just been the coastal strip, the beach cafés, the surf shops – it's all been ports: Port Isaac, Padstow, Polperro. I am part of the great emmet invasion that migrates to these shores between May and October. And, yes, it is easy to fall in love with the beaches and the thick August sunlight, Cornwall is held by the sea confounding and caressing one of the most beautiful coastlines in the world. But beyond the pull of the waves, beyond the dunes and the bearded coves and freed from the thunder of beauty, under the wrapping exists the fragility of something far more mysterious.

Trevigro, Cornwall

Start and finish: OS map 108. Grid reference 697338
Time: four hours

▶ From Trevigro take the very minor road that heads towards Callington up over the brow of a hill and then down into a wood.

▶ Cross the stream at the bottom and take the path on your immediate left. This leads through the wood and out into some fields. Here, it does become very confusing, but basically head up to your right towards a house called Woodland. There the path joins the minor road.

▶ Follow this road through Maders and South Hill and then on towards Linkinhorne. About half a mile before Linkinhorne you will see a path on your left, leading down through a field: take it. Make sure you look out for where the path heads into the field on your left, as this then leads down to a slippery bridge over a small stream.

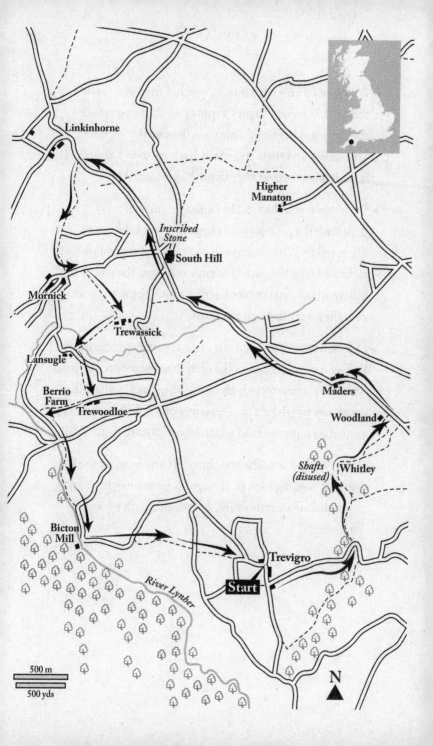

▸ Continue on this path into Mornick. When you reach
the road, turn left. Eighty yards or so further on, take
the path on your right. This runs diagonally down to
Trewassick and then diagonally back again to Lansugle. (I
hope the bridge over the stream has returned.)

▸ Once you reach the road in Lansugle, turn left and
then take the path on your right: this will take you to
Trewoodloe. When you reach the road in Trewoodloe turn
right and take the path that runs out from the end of the
village in the direction of Berrio Farm. I think the path
actually heads through the farm.

▸ Once through Berrio, go out on to the road and turn left.
Follow the road down to the end, then cross onto the path
which leads downwards alongside the River Lynher. This
continues for about three-quarters of a mile before being
funnelled onto the road which leads down to Bicton Mill.

▸ When you come to the end, turn left and head up the hill.
The path leading back to Trevigro is on your right, cutting
through a small stable yard. Follow this path back to
Trevigro.

Clyffe Pypard, Wiltshire

Walking with waves

I woke up and looking out of the window saw there were the tell-tale ferns of frost glued, it seemed, onto the flat felt roof below. It is only the fifth frost I have seen since the first one in November. The weather forecasters are already announcing that in southern England this January has been the wettest since records began in 1910; it has also, I am sure, been the warmest. The news channels are also warning us to stay away from the sea. In between the large areas of low-pressure that have been arriving this winter almost rhythmically one after the other from across the Atlantic ocean are small interludes of calm. But they never last long enough; nor is it warm enough for the sun to evaporate any of the water that has coalesced into the clouded brown lakes that now lie in the majority of the flatter fields of southern England.

The land cannot now absorb all the rain wrung from the clouds, creating mists of moisture that daze the distance, altering the appearance of the countryside completely and the water has been lying up for long enough to create a change in perception. It looks as if the sky has cracked, loosening large pieces that have fallen onto the fields. Huge flowing lakes have formed on the flooded land, which has shifted familiar patterns: squares become broken, hedges and trees emerge from a silver surface and no longer seem attached to the earth I thought I knew.

Clyffe Pypard is tucked right up against the side of a steep escarpment that reaches up to the plain of the Marlborough Downs. It had been a bright morning, but as I arrived and parked next to the pub a lost wind was turning anxious, rolling beech leaves over the road and shivering the hedges. Then almost without warning a deep grey cloud swung in from over the top of the escarpment and ambushed the village with heavy rain. It didn't last long, but it did enough to take me back to the car to put on some waterproof trousers. Waterproof trousers are not really either comfortable or practical: yes, they do keep the rain off your knees but that is the best I can say for them.

By the time I reached the church, which was no more than a hundred yards from where the car was parked, the rain had stopped. The churchyard was in places white with patches of snowdrops. Snowdrops are not indigenous to this country; it is thought they were first brought here by Benedictine monks and planted in the grounds of monasteries and abbeys. They used to be called 'Candlemas flowers' as they appear around the feast of Candlemas on 2 February. The flowers are symbols of purity and traditionally it has been considered unlucky to pick them and bring them inside. I have seen them covering the sides of steep wooded valleys in Devon and smothering the ground at Michelham Priory in Sussex. Snowdrops growing wild is usually an indication that at some point the land close by was once lived on.

The church was locked. I am still hoping to find more than one church in the countryside that is not being held to ransom by its apparent material value. The field beyond was being held hostage by the recent rains; it had been planted with grass, most of which was yellowing at the edges of the leaves and languishing in a grey mud that could not in any way support the weight of my steps. It was as if the land had had its skin removed, that I was walking on flesh, that the smaller veins near the surface had been torn and ripped by the plough and were utterly unable to filter the rain down through the soil. Each step was difficult, and the small grassed strip that formed the boundary between the next two fields and the path that led through them wasn't much easier. Other walkers had run their boots up along the edge of bramble patches to avoid slipping and sliding, to try and get a grip, but as the path narrowed I was left teetering on a sliver of bare earth between what had become a small pond on one side and a quagmire on the other.

When the sun returned it did so in a flash, varnishing the water lying on the land to the north, creating strands and pools of mercury and shining a new metal gateway that led into Broad Town. Standing in the garden of a house tucked under the base of escarpment to the south were the frames of two model deer; they were too far away for me to see whether they were made from chicken wire or willow. But not even the sunlight could brighten the sombre stance of several new houses, built using barely red bricks and brown window casings – a sea of daffodils would struggle to lift this. Maybe these houses have been intentionally designed so that nobody cares to look through the windows.

Broad Town doesn't really feel like a town at all; what I most liked about it were the dozen or so Brussels sprout plants taking a ragged stance in a raised border next to the parking area at the front of one of the houses. You don't see that many vegetables growing at the front of houses; vegetable patches tend to be dug right at the back of gardens. Much of this reality might have to do with the fact that there is still a little stone-age hard wiring left in all of us, the remnants of the hunter-gatherer, which calls us to pick anything edible whenever we see it and wherever it is. So the branches laden with apples, nuts, cherries and plums that happen to be just on the other side of the fence are always going to be tempting; but this temptation is no more than a natural desire. What is unnatural is that we should be forbidden from picking them. Is it really possible to own an apple?

The fences in the first of the fields beyond Broad Town looked as if they'd been conceived by the same mind that dreamed the sombre houses: a single wooden creosoted top piece under which was a hard metal mesh that had been run into the earth. The gates too leading from one field to another would not be out of place in a detention centre: great swinging bars of metal meshed at the base to stop people climbing over them. In any setting this is a form of brutality. Thankfully, on the other side of them is a fallow field, which I don't think has ever been ploughed. At some point long ago it may have been dug for clay, as the whole field is a series of small mounds, but it seemed very settled. What became immediately apparent was that, despite a few ready-made bowls and dips, there was no lying water: unlike the ploughed fields, the undisturbed land is self-draining so the underground veins taking the water in have not been broken. Some cattle however must have had a party in the bottom corner; not only had the earth turned to mush, but every indent and lying leaf seem preserved and was clearly visible beneath about eighteen inches of clear water. Underneath the water lay an utterly still world, untroubled, it would seem, by all the storms.

The hedges were too thick to find a way through, so I tightened my boots and said a prayer to the god of waterproof trousers and waded in. The one remaining dry leg didn't stay that way for long. The path entered a wood and turned into a deep mire of mud, curving and flowing around stands of long trunked trees planted in lines. In the sunlight their scored bark revealed greens and yellows at times hinting at flashes of purple, and the very few remaining leaves still sewn to the upper branches seemed released completely from the weight of purpose: sunlight always finds the colours hidden in a wood in winter. As the path led further into the wood it narrowed until eventually there was nothing left of it at all. It was meant to join another path that led to the top of the escarpment, so I simply headed north through the trees. On the ground there were signs of deer everywhere and the first lacquered green spikes of bluebells were pushing up through the earth. The waterproof trousers did come in handy as I rolled under a slack barbed-wire fence and jumped the ditch on the other side. Here the ground rose quite steeply into an old hazel coppice with a delightful collection of small, clear pools between three busy little white water streams that had cut their way into the bare black earth. It felt as if no one had been in here for many years; that I had stumbled into a secret. An old farm track appeared on the other side of the coppice but it was largely overgrown, with fronds of brambles crawling through the grass and the unruly beginnings of blackthorn trees.

The track wound towards the light then out into a soft, undulating field which leaned right into the base of the escarpment, the long wave rising over this part of Wiltshire. It is pretty much wooded from end to end and its symmetry is broken only by the remains of a few old quarries and some white scars of chalk. What should have been no more than a five-minute climb took twenty; at times the ground was so slippery that I took to kicking in footholds and clambering upwards using the side of my boots, hauling my way up by grabbing any available branch.

At the top there are two worlds.

The world I arrived in was a world of flattish fields and straight hedges but most of all a sudden expanse of sky: for the first time on the walk I had a 360-degree view of the horizon. The other world was the world that lay in the distance: the view looking north from the top must have extended ten miles or so – holding several large blocks of flats jutting up from the suburbs of Swindon, various woods, and a silent film of tiny cars and lorries floating in different directions and moving at different speeds across the land. Spreading south lay an expanse of the rounded hills which form the Marlborough Downs; at this time of year they are coloured somewhere between yellow, blue and grey and I love the stands of trees that seem to have been glued to the highest points of the hills. I knew that the village of Avebury lay close by.

I remember walking into it about twenty years ago, when it had been completely cut off at the time by a large snowfall. We arrived just before dusk and pitched our tents just to the side of one of the standing stone circles; that evening, we were the only people in the pub. Many of the standing stones at Avebury have either been restored or replaced, although a large number were broken up and used as building materials in the early eighteenth century: they were heated over a fire and then had cold water poured over them to crack them. By then the stones had been given Christian names: the Devil's Chair, the Devil's Quoits and the Devil's Brand Irons.

The upland areas of southern England such as the Marlborough Downs and my home on the South Downs still have burial chambers and tumuli in abundance. These relatively small pockets of elevated land still have an abidingly different melody about them, at once both more brutal and more beautiful. Both the South and Marlborough Downs feel as if they are not quite part of the world that carries on beneath them.

The path back to Clyffe Pypard runs right along the top edge of the escarpment, which is steep enough in most places to hide the slope itself, so at times it feels like a cliff edge. As I rounded the first corner two roe deer hinds jumped the escarpment fence and casually set about grazing on the winter wheat. I stood completely still and watched them for a while as they relaxed flicking their tails. Then one of them looked up and straight at me. She didn't move until I lifted my arm as a greeting – and at that point they both bolted.

About a quarter of a mile further on the aquiline young man who came walking towards me seemed a good deal more relaxed. He informed me that it was too dangerous to walk the path that led down the face of the escarpment because the recent rain had made the slope unstable and there could be landslides. I suggested this was probably the most exciting time to do it – a step at a time, listening for the movement of roots and the creaking of the earth. He looked at me as if I was speaking a completely foreign language, and then without a word he set off again. Maybe it was the creaking earth that frightened the fallow deer hind who leaped over the fence no more than ten feet in front of me; something had clearly upset her and she just carried on running at full pelt, on and on, without stopping and she kept running over the brow of the hill and I have no idea where she went from there.

Just beyond the road that leads down to Broad Town the path winds up through a scrubby piece of ground and past the bent remains of a corrugated iron shed that seemed to be in its final stages of form. It leads into a rather dreary field but from here the view begins to open out to the west. Looming on the horizon was another, this time almost circular, dark grey cloud, moving quickly towards me. Within about twenty seconds the wind grew frenzied; I could see the feathers of what I thought was rain swinging downwards from the base of the cloud and a minute later the hailstones arrived in ones and twos to begin with, then growing in intensity they battered the land. I was out in the open without the protection of trees, so I simply lay down and curled up on the ground. Hail is so much louder than rain, a rising crescendo of white noise, and it is almost alien: just the very reality that small and in some places large pieces of ice can fall from the sky, it is almost as strange as raining frogs and fish. On Titan, one of the moons of the planet Saturn, it rains liquid methane. Earth and Titan are the only planets in this solar system where it rains.

The hailstorm passed as quickly as it had arrived, leaving in its wake white puddles and footprints in the mud filled with crushed ice. The sun reappeared, colouring the land, turning the leafless elder trees standing alone into dark iron. I could have taken the path that cut down the side of the hill but the sunlit views were so dreamy that I was reluctant to let them go. It is a steep and dusky minor road that leads from the top of the plain back into Clyffe Pypard, winding down through the constant shade of mature beech trees. Being north facing, the escarpment slope would have a meagre helping of sunshine; the only trees standing in the light were at the top of the slope and in the sunlight their trunks had turned a rich luminous green.

A tree is a combination of so many things – earth and light, chlorophyll and sugar, oxygen and carbon, greys and greens. Each tree supports a multitude of life, from bacteria to buzzards. The very idea that it is a singular life form is bound up with the lonely science of separateness. Living on the skin on the underside of our elbows are five or six different types of bacteria and they are unique to that particular place on our bodies; without them the skin there would soon crack and weep. I cannot be alive without a host of other life forms living in symbiosis with me: they are me and I am them. At a gig in Brighton a couple of nights ago, the singer of the Trembling Bells expressed the reality of a living communion in this way, singing that 'beauty always comes with the imprint of pain'.

The Marlborough Downs really do feel like a plain, and walking the line between the plain and its hinterland beneath places you between worlds. Here the lines of separation become blurred – the separation between water and earth, yesterday and tomorrow, the deer and the woman, pink and blue. We are born between the lines of separation, lines that have been bequeathed by history and that we had no part in drawing – north and south, male and female, Somerset and Wiltshire, beech and elder, Christian and Muslim, God and man. So much time is spent negotiating the space between them. I am no longer convinced that any of that space actually exists; really, it is something we have just imagined. But the last seven weeks of storms have been real enough. They have come perhaps from the bitter fruit growing as a result of our having separated the present from the future.

Clyffe Pypard, Wiltshire

Start and finish: OS map 157. Grid reference 768074
Time: three hours

▶ The landlady of the Goddard Arms very kindly let me use
  the car park. From there, turn right and walk through the
  churchyard and you'll find that the path continues at the
  back of the church. This leads over several fields under the
  escarpment to Broad Town.

▶ When you reach the main street in Broad Town cross over
  and turn right, then first left, and carry on out of Broad
  Town along the White Horse Trail. The path here is not
  always easy to follow, but basically you need to keep to the
  land beneath the escarpment. This leads through the edge
  of some woods, but if you look carefully you will see the
  remains of a quarry carved into the hill.

▶ Keep walking until you come to what little is left of
  Bincknoll Castle. On the map here the White Horse Trail
  heads up the escarpment: follow it. Once on the top
  simply follow the path, which runs along the top edge of
  the escarpment all the way back. Although there is no
  path on the map, there is a path on the ground.

▶ When you reach the road that heads down the escarpment
  to Clyffe Pypard take it, and this will lead you back into
  the village.

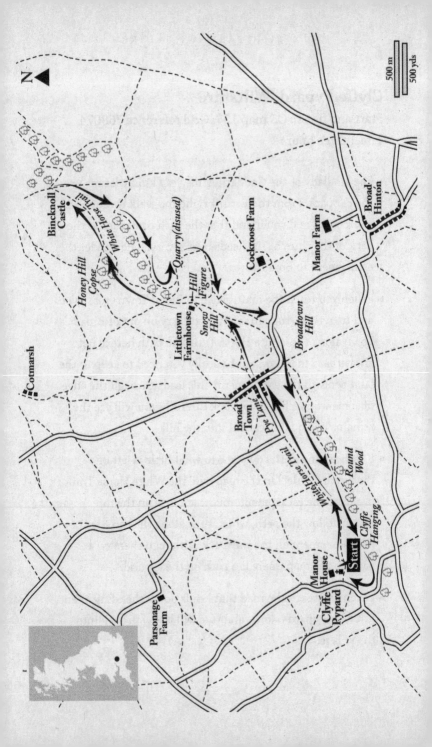

N

500 m
500 yds

Binknoll Castle

Broad Hinton

White Horse Trail

Honey Hill Copse

Quarry (disused)

Cockroost Farm

Manor Farm

Cotmarsh

Snow Hill Figure

Littletown Farmhouse

Broadtown Hill

Broad Town

Pye Lane

White Horse Trail

Round Wood

Cliffe Hanging

Start

Manor House

Clyffe Pypard

Parsonage Farm

Turville, the Chilterns

Deer and men

Winter is the time when certainties are tested. In winter I think about leaving and about what has been left behind; winter is the most mysterious of seasons – it is the time when the ghosts of beauty return. By mid-February the need of warmth becomes a hunger, this is when winter really kicks in: when we begin to endure it.

Turville sounds as if it should have a title in front of it: Admiral Charles or Sir Peregrine or the Revd Rodney. The village sits right on the floor of a valley and, driving above it, it could easily be mistaken for a large farm, but there is a pub and a squat grey church and an almost round little village green which must be just slightly bigger than a parachute. It wasn't hard to imagine the slender Revd Rodney Turville, dressed in black and sporting a low-crowned bowler hat, walking purposefully between the red-brick and flint houses with a book in one hand and a cane in the other, but those days are gone.

The forecast had promised sunshine after midday, but there was no mention of the fine drizzle that doesn't really fall, it appears to float, and when there is a monkeys' wedding – when there is sunshine and rain at the same time – every previously invisible droplet reflects the light and turns into glitter. The sunshine seemed a long way off, the wooded tops of the valleys smoking with swirls of low cloud that every so often would thicken and fill the distance with dust.

The path out of Turville heads up from the village green between some houses, where a boy was kicking a ball against wooden garage doors. It was half-term and he seemed so alone that I said good morning and he just looked at me. Beyond the houses the path turns into a black stew and enters a tunnel, a bower made of thin elders and thorns, which opens out into an eaten field where a few sheep were gleaning what little was left of some winter turnips.

Just before the path crosses a minor road and leads quite steeply uphill, a couple of dogs were running along behind the new wooden fence of a house next to the road, barking and snarling. They couldn't see me; they must have picked up my scent. It is always sobering to sense hostility, to be aware of how it pulls the triggers of immediate reality and folds your fingers into your palms, forcing men in particular to confront one of their greatest fears, which is the fear of being a coward. Those who keep aggressive dogs are really telling you that they are afraid.

Rather strangely, the path turns into a wide swathe of concrete in the middle of a bedraggled wood that runs up to South End Farm. It must have been laid to give the tractors grip as they pulled up and down the side of this valley. Tractors have increased in size over the years, adding cabs, air conditioning, weight, horsepower and music systems, but in the absence of concrete, horsepower would have fared much better. It is all very well to buy a spanking new nine and a half ton tractor but if it is too heavy to make it through the mud you will be spending the same again on concrete. On the other side of the wood I could hear Marvin Gaye and Tammi Terrell singing 'All the joys under the sun wrapped up into one, you're all I need to get by', their voices drifting over the fields from the music system of an open van, parked in the yard of South End Farm. It wasn't incongruous, a duet blended so beautifully in Detroit in the sixties singing through the winter trees of England in the twenty-first century. What did seem out of place was the row of new-build barns, rectangles of steel and iron, one following the other in mathematical order, and a plethora of yellow and black signs strung on the gates, nailed into walls: there were too many rules to read.

The footpath sign that points over the fields to Summerheath Wood wasn't far beyond the farm and, as I clambered over the stile, a flight of wood pigeons rose from the ground and floated in front of a stand of grey trees. Something wonderful happens to wood pigeons in February and March; they shed the cumbersome, they seem to slow down and become delicate and, from a distance, in the air they look like large butterflies. Wood pigeon chicks are called squabs and in eight weeks or so the females would be sitting on their first clutch of eggs.

I must have been about nine or ten, and had been bowled

out for a duck in a game of garden cricket that the family I was staying with were taking far too seriously. So I crept into the woods and climbed a pine tree. I could see a bundle of twigs above me, I just had to climb around it. Sitting on top of it were two of the most fabulously grotesque creatures I have ever seen to this day. They were wood pigeon chicks covered in feather casings that appeared to be spines and they stared at me with faces borrowed from frogs and dodos, they had hooked bills, bulbous eyes and a halo of flies. We looked at each other and perhaps thought the same thing.

Just before the path enters Summerheath Wood it crosses the top of a sloping field with views south over the wooded tops of seemingly unending hills. I have never been to the Chilterns before. They don't feel intensively cultivated but even with red kites hanging over the valleys in twos and threes seeing the secrets they keep, they don't feel wild; yet the Chilterns feel as if they harbour secrets. There was no such mystery about the wooden sign at the side of the stile leading into the wood. It told me that 'the woodland is managed for wildlife and biodiversity'. Ten yards further on another sign was pinned to a tree. This one read 'Overhanging tree, proceed with caution, avoid if possible'. Surely all trees are overhanging? But my favourite was a couple of hundred yards further on; sprayed in black onto the grey trunk of a tall sycamore, it simply said 'Squirrels this way' and underneath it someone had kindly added an arrow pointing upwards. In fact, in this wood there are arrows every twenty yards or so – white ones, painted on the trees just above head height. They are clearly here to encourage those of us walking through the wood to stay on the path, or maybe they remain as a testament to an organised walk, but really it was as if the woodland had been defaced, as if this one action compromised not only the naturalness of the wood but also a sense of naturalness you feel within it.

Nothing seemed to be bothering the birds, though; the songs of great tits, blue tits, blackbirds and chaffinches were throbbing through the tall trees. Tall trees have a gentleness about them, a patience, they exude calm. When an elderly Taoist monk in China was trying to explain to me that I should accept, without resistance, all that I experienced as being painful and challenging he used the metaphor of a tree. He must have been in his eighties and he jumped on to a chair and joined his hands together above his head. Bending forward and sideways, one movement flowing into another, he said: 'Go with it, Peter, the tree does not resist the way of the wind.'

I imagined he would have loved the half-finished camp and the swing strung on blue nylon rope that hung next to it. I had stumbled into a private world, a half-made frame of various sticks propped around the trunk of an oak. Scattered in front of it was a drift of snowdrops and some way further on the beginnings of a back garden. The promised sun then rushed in and suddenly I was seven again, sitting on a warm earth floor under the triangular stems of broken bracken spreading crushed raspberries onto stolen slices of white bread.

The teenagers walking up the road beyond the camp were trudging rather than walking. As they approached, I asked their father whether they always walked as a family and he replied in a rather world-weary fashion that it was half-term and walking with them was the only way he could get any peace. Their mother said nothing. Maybe they had had an argument, as they laboured straight past a wild cherry tree frilling with white and scarlet blossoms without even looking at it.

The hedge that sits at the front of Turville Grange stopped me in my tracks: it is the most beautiful hedge I have ever seen. It seems to have been sculpted out of seawater, an evolution of a rough wave, folding light evergreen layers into curving and bowing non-symmetrical surfaces creating one exquisite form, it is achingly sensuous. As I was standing there admiring it, a woman started to sing; there were no words in her song, just a loose collection of notes rising from somewhere on the other side of the hedge. The next couple of hundred yards were a bit of a blur as I wandered down towards Turville Court but the spell was broken by the tight and overwhelming order of the place and a handful more yellow and black signs saying that Alsatians had the run of the land on the other side of the gates.

After a slightly tense walk between the stable yard and the house, I followed the path down the back of Turville Court, where a large iron bird spreads its wings on top of a plinth. As more fine drizzle came in I crossed the field down into a steep-sided wood, where steps had kindly been cut into the earth; without them it would not have been an easy descent. On the other side of the wood the drizzle had cleared and Manor Farm appeared. Perched almost on top of the opposite hill, it looked more like a bank than a farm, as if it were part of a collection of buildings that formed a high street sitting next to the tracks of an electric train set. Beneath it, a lone red traffic light shone through the mix of a hedge, but there were no road works and, like the farm that looked like a bank, the light seemed completely out of place. The red traffic light was part of an automated entrance system but there was no indication of what lay beyond it.

As I looked down from the path that climbs the hill, which holds a quite beautiful valley, I could only see a distant collection of new barns, where a group of men had gathered in a cloud of smoke around a Land Rover. There wasn't much more to see of Manor Farm. The slope is steep enough to hide the house so all that is really visible is chimneys, and once the trees are in leaf they will be gone.

I had missed the single thinly inked cross on the map and so the graveyard that began to appear through the trees and St Nicholas's church came as a complete surprise. It is a church on its own, built into the most prominent position overlooking the valley but now almost encased in trees. The stones felt old and borrowed, as if the church had been cobbled together from the remains of various ages. I turned the handle and the door opened. English country churches have a unique scent, a mix of polish, old books and snuffed candles. So many churches end up imprisoned by their history, contained in tidiness, but they were never meant to be keepers of history, least of all their own. This one felt like a house of dreams. It is tiny, more like a couple of rooms in a summerhouse. If there had been a beaten-up sofa in the corner and some old teddy bears lounging on the cushions they wouldn't have looked at all out of place. There are only five or six rows of pews and what lay in the chancel seemed veiled and impossible to name.

I signed the visitors' book and went to sit on one of the bench seats in the porch. And minute or so later Karen and her dog, Pippin, came walking through the graveyard and we got talking. She said that most of the land close by was owned by the Getty family and pointed to a large sandstone house on the other side of the valley; that there was a hanging tree up on Ibstone Common and a dead fawn lying at the side of road on the way into the village; also that a wandering monk had sworn an oath that he would not rest until unhindered access along the footpaths around the church was guaranteed to all by the then Lord of the Manor. She didn't say whether the monk was able to rest in peace or not, but the path up from the church heading towards Ibstone has certainly been trodden for many centuries.

On the path down from the ridge a group of men were putting up a deer fence. The largest of them confessed he had a lurcher that could bring down any deer, and that good venison should not be wasted. There didn't appear much chance of any deer managing to breach these new defences and I would rather live with the deer than the fence. At the bottom of the hill it began to rain as the path swings into a pinewood. On the ground the remains of thinner trees lay tattered in various lengths; some machines must have been in clearing out any trees that weren't considered to be economically viable to grow on.

In the south-west corner of Crete, growing out of the white sand just above the shoreline of a small sliver of a bay, stands an old juniper forest. It looks over an aquamarine sea where silver fish dart and breathe between the small summer waves and from late morning until late afternoon the scent within the trees is sweet and heady. But in England in the February rain these lines of planted pines are so serious, they seem to thrive on sorrow.

On the other side of the wood the path follows the valley floor and yet more white arrows but just about the entire length of it had been stirred by horses and was ankle deep in mud. Weaving alongside it is a winter path that turns and winds through a thin band of elders and grasping bramble stems; I would imagine that in the summer, when the mud has set hard, it isn't needed. After about a mile the elders and brambles come to an end. And there, grazing in the distance just in front of a wood, was a single deer: it was a hind, but it was too far away for me to tell whether it was a roe or a fallow. I saw no other deer apart from that one, and very few hoof prints.

What is impossible to miss is Cobstone windmill. It sits almost on the top of the hill above Turville and the path back down into the village runs straight past it. It was rebuilt in the sixties and used as the location for the home of the inventor Caractacus Potts in the film *Chitty Chitty Bang Bang*. It must have been having another refit, as it was swallowed up by scaffolding. From the windmill looking down over Turville, an ornate white summerhouse stands out in the far corner of a garden on the opposite hill, looking like another part of the set from *Chitty Chitty Bang Bang* – the top of the watchtower of the castle sitting on top of the hill in the fictional land of Vulgaria.

I am not sure what the fourteen red kites who were

trawling the air just beyond the ridge were looking out for: they are expensive birds, flying princes. It was only when I sat down in the car and rolled a cigarette before turning the engine on that I realised I had had so very little privacy during this walk; for most of it I could have been observed from the windows of the big houses that look out across the valleys.

I had gone searching for spring but I hadn't found it. Not yet – but I had heard it. It was rising in the tone of the woman's voice singing behind the hedge; and just before I entered Summerheath Wood a thin mist had come in, washing the colour out of the fields and the definition out of the distance, and from within the mist a single invisible male skylark sang. Scientists might tell me that gravity is the strongest force in the universe; the Revd Rodney Turville might quietly implore that it is love. Perhaps it is neither of these things. The strongest force in the universe is surely desire.

Turville, The Chilterns

Start and finish: OS map 171. Grid reference 913768
Time: four hours

▶ From the village green in Turville, take the path that heads south-west out of the village (the Chiltern Way). Follow this for about a mile until you reach a minor road.

▶ Cross the road and take the path opposite. From here the path heads uphill and on to a concrete track, which leads to South End Farm.

▶ Once past South End Farm, take the first path on your right: this runs over some fields and then enters Summerheath Wood. The path here is marked with arrows on the trees. Head for the corner of the wood where the path emerges on to a minor road. Here turn left and then take the first path on your right.

▶ Follow it up to Turville Grange. Walk through the Grange. The path then bears sharp left and runs down along the back of the Grange gardens, then over a field and into a wood. Follow the path through the wood, down some steps, and then across another field until you reach the minor road called Holloway Lane.

▶ The path you need is almost opposite. Take it and veer to the left, following the route up and out of the wood and then across a field, which runs underneath Manor Farm.

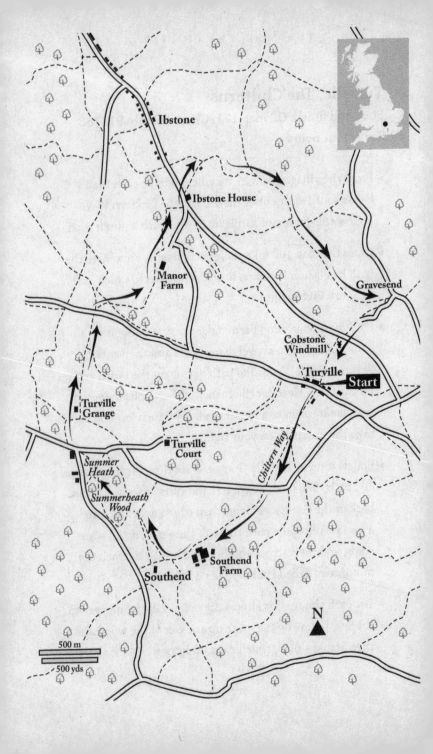

▸ The path cuts round the edge of the farm and rises up steeply to St Nicholas's Church. The path then continues from the churchyard, heading north.

▸ Keep going for about half a mile and then take the first path on your right, which will take you to Ibstone. Once you reach the road, turn left and walk past the little school and then take the path on your right. This heads down into quite a deep valley.

▸ Just before the bottom of the valley take the path on your right, which runs through a small wood before following the valley floor.

▸ Continue along the valley floor for a couple of miles or so, then take the path on your right, which almost doubles back on the route. This path will take you up to the road and the windmill.

▸ From the windmill follow the path down into the valley, which is quite steep in places, and back into Turville.

Castle Acre, Norfolk

Smoke and sky

I can't quite work out how Castle Acre happened. It is just a wide street with a grassed area between the facing houses. Maybe in the past most of the grass was front gardens or maybe it has always been this wide – a space holding trees and pulsing birdsong. What is diminished in this breadth is the road leading through the main street of Castle Acre: it does not define the space, it sits within it; it is just a part of the mix of branches, old bricks and windows.

I love arriving in a village where the first and, at the time, most natural thing to do when I get out of the car is to take a deep breath: that almost unconscious response, which only happens when you arrive in a place perfectly at ease with its existence, and you breathe that in. You take in the change of colour, of light and scent; but perhaps what is really happening when we do this is that we are gauging the atmosphere: we are feeling how the place feels. Each home and street, each wood and mountain – every city, church and mosque and river: they all have their own resonance. Castle Acre feels gentle.

Winter is under siege now, there are days when she still breaks out and taunts the maidens of daffodils lining up along the roadsides, and rides in on the remains of cold skies, cursing the extravagance of blossom and the first parties of cluster flies jiving in any sunlight they can find. But by mid-March the sunshine is softening, the rooks have built their cities high in trees, the vixens have given birth and are suckling their cubs. Song thrushes are lining their nests with mud and when it has set the female will lay three to five blue eggs that have surely been stolen from a sweet-shop window. On the way towards Castle Acre, the willows sitting on the banks of the dykes in the Fens could have been made out of a peach-coloured candy. Spring is such a heady mixture of milk and sugar.

In Castle Acre, a cherry tree was in full blossom just inside the entrance to a large house near the church; beneath the tree were handfuls of primroses. This pink and yellow picture was a page from a children's book: the place where the story begins and is bound to end. A hundred yards or so from the cherry tree, two men were grappling with individual flints and mortar, rebuilding a lone and untidy section of the wall that surrounds the remains of Castle Acre Priory. The foundations of the priory were laid in 1087 and it was just one of over thirty Cluniac priories built in England and Wales after the Norman Conquest as part of William's master plan to bring the full force of God down on the English and Welsh.

The conquest of England in 1066 was as much of a land grab as a crusade. Or perhaps the latter provided the justification as it has done all too often for the former? Norman society was underpinned by three interdependent divisions of labour, each of which was there to serve the other. After the Norman Conquest, the only choices you would have had were to pray, to fight or to work. Those who did the praying arrived from France several years after England had been subdued. The first of the new priories was built in my home town of Lewes and the abbot of what was to become Castle Acre Priory reported directly to the abbot of Lewes Priory. Now all that remains of both priories are sections of broken walls, glassless windows and pieces of stories. It always seems strange to tend the remains of buildings, and the two men standing on a platform next to a large blue plastic tarpaulin were surely building a new wall as much as restoring an old one. I asked one of them how far he reckoned it was to West Acre. 'It's about two and half miles,' he replied. Then he added, 'It's a lovely day for it.'

It was. The sun was waning a little under thickening white wisps of cloud, but it wasn't cold. It was warm enough to wake the first of the bumblebee queens, who were drifting content-edly along the bottom of hedgerows, filling up on enough nectar to give them the energy to lay their first brood, who were destined to be workers and fighters; only the bumblebee queens survive the winter.

For the first time since November the paths were dry; there were occasional puddles and swirls of mud, but for the most part it wasn't slippery any more. The monks of Castle Acre must have surely walked through this valley, which sinks into the land from the southern end of the village to West

Acre where another, much smaller, priory was built. From Castle Acre the valley leads down out of the village in between two high hedges where the first frills of new green leaves were emerging. At the foot of the slope is a large marshy area thick with willows and the creamy coloured strands of last year's rushes. It was criss-crossed with the tracks of a bulldozer and leading into it was a rickety walkway laid from various lengths of unrelated planks, slung across the mire and wobbling onto the bank of the River Nar. I know that further downstream the river holds brown trout and slips through woods, where once on a hot July day I took off all my clothes and lay in the lazy current. But in March it is fast with fresh rain, it is youthful: running cold and clear beckoning old men to remember.

Once past the marsh the land opened out and the path meandered alongside a great bowl of sedge and, within it, a couple of small clumps of willow encircled by bulrushes stood guard over these unreachable islands. I loved the fact that they were out of reach, that they could be seen but not known, neither the intermingling branches of willow nor the deep nests of moorhens woven from the long leaves of rushes. In England, there may still be a few places which human beings have not yet trodden or handled, but I would imagine they can be measured in paces and yards – maybe a ledge in the Lake District high up on the Langdale Pikes, or the low tide lands running under the great cliffs on either side of Hartland Point in Devon. But surely something has been missed, something utterly incidental like a clump of willows in the middle of acres of sedge?

The path leading to West Acre is well trodden as it forms a part of the Nar Valley Way, which arrived on the maps in the 1990s. These waymarked walks are generally longer than strolls: the Nar Valley Way runs for over thirty miles. It starts, or ends, at the Farm and Workhouse Museum in Gressenhall and runs into King's Lynn, passing under a road bridge where the banks of the river have hardened into concrete and the walls beneath the traffic are caked in graffiti. These waymarked walks feel more public – the paths are generally wider, the stiles are a lot less rickety – and on the weekends they often bubble with conversation and the names of dogs being called out loud. On a Monday afternoon the path was empty except for a few jackdaws and the occasional brown blur of a wren. I had the sun melting the river into silver all to myself.

After about three-quarters of a mile or so the sedge releases the river as it flows into a wood of oaks and sycamores and sinks out of sight. Here the path straightens and follows the edge of the wood. In the field next to it a raucous gaggle of greylag geese stood shouting at each other, while nearer the fence a small group of Red Lincoln mothers were tending their polished calves. I leaned on the fence for a while, watching more geese coming in to land in threes and fours, and one young calf, who, despite the obvious concern of his mother, gingerly edged towards me, juggling the need to explore with the fear of what he might find. The Desert Fathers, the monks living on bread and air in the lunar landscape of the Sinai Desert, consciously embraced fear to find freedom from it: it is the first doorway leading into the house with many rooms.

In another open room by the side of the path, a still swing

hung down from a ceiling of branches. Underneath it the ground had been scuffed, but the rope and the wood looked new so I sat down and took off. On the north-west corner of the island of St Martin's in the Scilly Isles someone has strung a hammock made from a washed-up fishing net between two pines just above a white sand cove. Like the swing, it is a random act of kindness, an anonymous gift given by one human being to a whole host of people they are unlikely ever to meet, it is one of the sweetest forms of generosity. As the path arrived in West Acre the unmistakable aroma of sausages filled the air, conjured up from the other side of the footbridge crossing a river flashing with sparks.

On the other side of the bridge, the path leads over a road and heads down between some tilting trees to a ford as round as a pond. Three teenagers were sitting on the banks above the water, saturated in the unruly smoke of an instant barbecue. Around them lay torn-open packets of bargain beef burgers, white rolls and various different shades of sausages. Teenagers out in the countryside, in woods and fields and hanging out around fords, are becoming as rare as tree sparrows. I wandered down to the ford and said hello and suggested it was a great location for a barbecue, and asked how often they ate outside. Their names were Sam, Chris and Hannah and I felt I knew them: at least I knew what it was like to be a teenager living in a village in the English countryside, that was then. Now there is the internet, Facebook and mobile phones but the basics haven't changed much: the same faces are propped up in the same pubs and if you want to go anywhere it means your parents have to take you there. Nightclubs, cinemas and football stadiums are all essentially out of reach so you must create your own entertainment, like racking up a barbecue on a March afternoon on the banks of a nearby ford. And I admired them for that. As I wandered back up towards the path one of them shouted out, 'Hey, do you want a sausage?' and they very kindly unrolled a piece of kitchen towel and placed an ebony black chipolata in one of the beef-burger boxes. It was only then I realised they didn't have a knife or a fork between them.

Up from the ford the path rises slightly and straightens along the edge of a small piece of heathland. Here the earth turns loose and sandy, the gorse thirsts and the only vivid colour on that March day was the yellow of one small stand of lost daffodils. What grass there was had been shorn by rabbits, who only appeared when they moved. Other than that, they became invisible in the camouflage of the meagre grey wood.

The ruins of West Acre Priory lie behind the trees just before the path turns north, a leaden collection of stones rising up out of yet more sedge. It was impossible for monks and nuns to buy land so they were given it either by the fighters or the workers. Most of that land is what is now disparagingly called 'low grade land', parcels of swamp or a few acres of estuary mud. This suited both parties: the benefactors bought their way into heaven and the monks and nuns could build their castles, priories and abbeys, from where they searched, for hundreds of years, for the paradise surrounding them.

Not half a mile from what is left of West Acre Priory is a mound of land covered in trees. A priory here would have been protected from the malaria-carrying mosquitoes and thick damp of the marshlands. North Norfolk is peppered with these mounds, very few of which have been built on; there is one near Cley next the Sea that in six weeks' time or so, when the bluebells flower, will turn the colour of a summer sky.

In pre-Reformation England, hares would have been a common sight. But the two that sprang from the field leading up to the mound made for a sight that's becoming increasingly rare. The last time I saw more than one hare was three years ago on the west coast of Ireland: they had taken to the rocks leading down to the wild edges of Dog's Bay in Galway. There must be millions of hares on the front of greetings cards, mugs, tea towels and doormats – most homes probably have the image of a hare somewhere within them – but out in the countryside their numbers continue to plummet. Along with eagles, robins and deer, hares are cast as the folk heroes of the natural world, they are totems of fertility and femininity, but they have succumbed to the more powerful spell of marketing. As I watched them run over the brow of the field leading to the mound they became fluid and ghostly. It is this quality that the priests of the past believed demonstrated that hares could cross the line between the flesh and the spirit.

Having left the Nar Valley Way, I crossed the line between the public and the intimate, between thinking and being. As the land rises gently the sky widens over the ridge above the valley where the path leans first south and then east, heading along the edges of fields and under the branches of oaks. Here the ground isn't patterned with footprints, the pheasants I saw scarpered, and a pair of great spotted woodpeckers bounced through the air between trees. I was back in the pathlands on the barely walked trails. Here I am not walking through the land – I am led into it: into the call of the distance and the still worlds of detail. It was my shadow that woke me, suddenly walking along in front of me as the sun broke through what had become a ceiling of cloud, the light crushed between the sky and the land swelling the sycamore buds and casting a long line of trees into black silhouettes.

By the time I reached Saint Nicholas's church in South Acre a deep magenta red line stretched from one end of the western horizon to the other and suddenly the sky became thrilling. The church windows were boarded up and the graveyard was thin on tombstones: it seemed strangely empty. Nothing has been done at the back of the church to make it pretty, to define it; there isn't a flint wall or a clipped hedge separating the graveyard from the field in front of it. If the slackened barbed-wire fence hadn't been there, it would have been almost impossible to know where the farmland begins and the consecrated land ends: this remains a dreadful division. Floating on the far side of the hedge up from the church was the glimpse of a barn owl's wings. These owls usually appear just before dusk and they fly silently. In a couple of weeks' time the female will lay her pure white eggs. Unlike most birds, she broods them as she lays them, so there is a gap of two to three days between the arrival of each chick. Often, the last one to hatch does not survive. A barn owl chick can swallow up to twelve mice a night.

The light was fading as I reached Castle Acre and I tried to cut up through the back of the remnants of the monastery, but there was no way across a large ditch whispering with rushes so I returned through the long grass to the blackening water of the River Nar. As I made my way up the hill towards the centre of the village I wondered what the teenagers were doing. Perhaps they were still sitting on the banks of the ford. Those instant barbecues do not burn for very long so maybe they had made their way home and were back in their bedrooms looking into a screen, talking to their friends on Facebook, their hair reeking of beef burgers and charcoal. In three or four hours' time they would fall asleep in a world without sirens and car horns and the rumbling of a city in which one day they might live for a while. Or maybe they were still there on the banks of that round ford, their faces lighting up and bending with each drag they took on their cigarettes. Maybe they noticed the first emerging bats looping in to hunt over the water; and much later on they would walk up along the dark lane, not knowing that to make the same journey in ten years' time will bring them such comfort.

Castle Acre, Norfolk

Start and finish: OS map 236. Grid reference 817152
Time: three hours

▶ From the main street in Castle Acre, head south past the church and the remains of the priory wall. At the end of the wall turn right and about a couple of hundred yards further on turn left, then follow the path downhill into the Nar Valley. This path (part of the Nar Valley Way) takes you towards West Acre.

▶ Before you reach West Acre, the path crosses two bridges and then a road skirting along the edge of a small common. Cross the common and just before West Acre take the path on your left, which runs alongside a hedge. This leads to a road: cross it and continue to head south, following the path up on to the ridge.

▶ Once you reach the brow of the ridge turn left and follow the path through the fields for a mile and a half or so. Then take the path on your left: this is a wide path called Petticoat Drove, which leads down to the road. Here you should turn right.

▶ Once past St George's Church, take the route on your left: this leads past Church Farm. From here follow the path over the ford and back up into Castle Acre, where there is a very fine pub indeed.

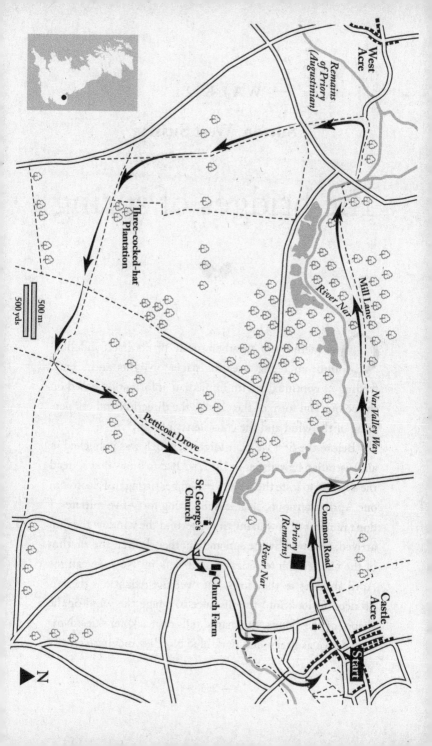

Sutton, West Sussex

The bridges of spring

Our memory of weather surely prints itself indelibly into our being, creating pages of lights and scents, feeding us continually with immediate information based on the colour and form of the clouds, the direction and temperature of the wind and the consistency of light.

Before the first weather forecast, which was published in an Australian newspaper in 1877, we had to know how to read the sky, and to taste the wind. I remember sitting in a classroom one April afternoon, each lesson lasting forty-five minutes. I don't remember how many times beyond the window the rain arrived, followed by the sun and another shower, the rhythm of the changing intensities of light sank in. Now we can see April showers as they form out over the Atlantic – there is no need to look into the distance to gauge the wind or the shapes of the clouds, the mares' tails or mackerel skies. Now they arrive as green and dark blue blotches moving across a sand- coloured land on a computer screen.

Here, everything was new. The edges of the path walking out of Sutton were packed tight with leaves jostling to be seen. Uncultivated land has no plan, it just happens: the shapes and colours of the verges are conceived in part by the force of autumn winds scattering seeds and the ferocity of frosts culling all pretenders. New leaves hold the rain; they only begin to harden on hot days and by midsummer they have set like wax. But right now, in the third quarter of April, they are still being born: they are without muscles or sap and appear to be sleeping. Each year a healthy fully grown oak will produce up to 250,000 leaves, each one turning sunshine into sugar.

Today, there was apparently going to be some sunshine, but the wooded slopes of the South Downs that rise just beyond the village were guarded by hovering layers of cloud; at a quarter to eight in the morning the air was heavy and damp with last night's rain holding all the birdsong. The summer migrants are now arriving – chiffchaffs, blackcaps, garden and grasshopper warblers – and the resident thrushes, blackbirds, robins, tits and wrens are also singing their hearts out. At this time of year, blackbirds and thrushes begin to sing just before the first shards of dawn become visible.

As I entered adolescence, I would wake at around two in the morning. It was my first prolonged encounter with terror. I would lie there on a single metal-framed bed in a dormitory that contained another fourteen beds, terrified that my heart would stop beating. I waited each night for the end that I nearly convinced myself was certain. I would only relax and fall back to sleep once I had heard the first bird sing. It remains

– this song in the dark – one of the most glorious responses to existence.

The wild garlic was in full voice, carpeting over every inch of earth and filling the air with French sweat in a rugged little copse about half a mile from the village of Sutton. I loved the fact that rather than walk the path alongside it, others had trodden a rough winding line through the middle of it; others had come this way just to breathe it all in. When the path petered out I waded through the white flowers and jumped the ditch to re-join the main path and wandered on, passing bluebells growing among pasture, milkmaids, primroses and the coy first flowers of red campion. A great swirl of mist infused with light came and went just before Barlavington, where very sadly the little church of St Mary's was locked. I did try peering in, but the glass in the lower windows is thickened with yellows and greens, turning the interior watery and shapeless.

Standing next to the path leading away out from Barlavington is a yew tree with the widest girth I have ever seen. The trunk is the size of a stable, the bark rutted and peeling in variegated lines of creams, greys and browns peppered with blackened holes that were twisting their way inwards. As the air warmed it sweetened and a pair of swallows flashed over a field spiked with tufts of soft rush and one or two lush vagrant dock leaves. I wasn't expecting the waterfall that tipped evenly into a deep pool just on the edge of a small wood that led into Burton Park. It was built so tenderly, a low semi-circular tunnel under which leans a flat rippling base unfolding into a white veil of water. There is nothing grand about it; it sits naturally and easily in the land. It isn't announced in any way. The landscape often turns bleak around large country houses. In the past, these mansions were in themselves small villages, some employing hundreds of people – butlers, housekeepers, cooks, grooms, drivers, gardeners, valets, ladies' maids, housemaids and more: they were buzzing with activity. Now, unless they have become tourist attractions, they feel empty and forsaken, they are the homes of lost echoes.

The land around many of these stately homes was shaped by Lancelot 'Capability' Brown and other landscape architects; they left a cold legacy. They scoured out ivy and bryony, dug up the brambles, had the moles murdered, shot the wild flowers and, arranged the trees as if they were on a church window, they turned paradise pale. I saw the big house – a magnolia cube – from the low little hill just beyond Sutton. On the map the proportions of the lake had been cut out of graph paper, so once past the waterfall I knew I would be entering the land of lonely trees, only redeemed by a few idiosyncrasies, maybe the odd stone griffin or a herd of fallow deer flicking their tails.

The white alpacas were a surprise: there were only two of them, blending in with the sheep grazing behind the curving iron fence that swept towards Burton Park. The picture on the front of the *Guide to Burton Church* gives the impression that the church is bigger than Burton Park House when in reality it is surely smaller than the kitchen. The handle of the door to St Richard's Church opened into a room that felt like the attic at the top of a large house, the attic room where the last teenage inhabitant had travelled the rites of passage between the girl and the woman, and who in the warm stoned nights had painted the walls with the visions of her journey. The most vivid of the murals here is of a young woman tied spread-eagled onto two planks of wood. She is hanging upside down, with her long red hair falling down on to a frame of repeating triangles. The mural of the Stuart coat of arms is delightfully unfinished but the chilling inscription above it is still very readable: 'Obey them that have the rule over you.' Underneath it is dated 1636. Having signed the visitors' book, I sat on the porch, watching some swallows going where they pleased.

From Burton, the path leads into a delightfully dishevelled wood. It looked as though this might have been the main thoroughfare to the house at some point, running between an avenue of huge cream-trunked trees that are clearly struggling now. Beyond them a fox sauntered across the path; I thought he had long gone but he was there waiting, standing in front of a small clump of dark-leafed rhododendrons and staring directly at me. I smiled, raised my hat and said good morning, but I was not to be trusted and after about twenty seconds he turned and slipped into the undergrowth without moving a leaf.

An incongruous tarmac path led through the wood, but it was crumbling and covered in beech mast. On the north side the land slopes up through occasional pines and a thick carpet of bracken. On the south it sinks into black bogs and tangles of fallen branches fermenting frenzied smears of cluster flies shaking the air. Then through it came the unmistakable notes of a cuckoo: I love how their call sounds as if it is coming from every direction. How it smothers its way over every other bird's song and sinks into thickets and vales. It is only the males that call, and they only do it when they arrive here in their breeding season: in Africa they are silent. But here, on a sub-tropical spring morning when the sun is heaving down the first flush of heat, rousing slumbering leaves and stirring scents, the male cuckoo thickens the air just enough to hide his intentions.

A couple of years ago I spent a day in Kingley Vale, Europe's largest yew forest, which is about twenty miles or so from Sutton. The warden stood in the car park and called in a cuckoo. He had heard the male calling and stood there with his hands around his mouth, mimicking the call. Sure enough, some two minutes later the cuckoo flew in and hopped through the branches of a horse chestnut to get a better view of his rival. Cuckoos are solitary birds.

A commotion of gulls were arguing in the sky just above the large millpond holding on to the sky in front of Burton Mill, where the water folds down under the road and swings away beneath some trees. From here, the minor road sloped slightly uphill through the edge of a wood, which was lit with bluebells and clumps of primroses. There was nothing to indicate that a path crossed the meadow on the other side of the stile languishing in the hedge. No one had left their darker green footprints in the dew. The path is there on paper but was lost on the ground under rising spring grasses and the first shining buttercups.

By the time I reached the stile in the far corner my socks were sodden and my boots had turned dark brown. In April, there is often not enough heat during the day to melt away the morning dew or to shrink the long puddles in the ruts of the farm track leading towards Coates. Here, the path is more of a border that exists between two worlds. To my left lay acres of land where nothing was thriving apart from a uniform smothering of silage grass, every blade the same height and same shade of green. To my right, the land rose in mounds, little hillocks each supporting a handful of silver birches, willows and thorns in the first laces of new leaves. There was movement here: on the ground red-legged partridges and blackbirds gleaned through the leaf litter, songbirds darted from tree to tree, all of them scattering when a red deer hind ran off in a panic, forcing a lumbering buzzard to stagger upwards between the trees.

Fifteen years after the chilling inscription was written above the Stuart coat of arms in St Richard's Church in Burton, Thomas Hobbes wrote in *Leviathan*, even more chillingly, that the life of a man is solitary, poor, nasty, brutish and short. His words ushered in a state of spiritual paralysis that eventually ended up in the ink on the licence to disenchant the land and crown us all kings over sparrows.

I didn't see the driver of the ruddy great tractor that bellowed up the track and it was long gone by the time I reached Coates Lane, which leads up to Sutton Common. The green paint was peeling on the board by the side of the lane that announced St Agatha's Church. This little church sits almost in a field, in among grasses and overgrown hedges, inside it is plain and beautiful.

I think it was a male goldcrest I saw in the churchyard, flitting around in the hedge: he flew off and then returned, landing about three feet away hopping precisely from twig to twig. Whilst the goldcrest is classified as the smallest British bird, the long-tailed tit has a smaller skeleton. Both lay the most exquisite tiny white and pink eggs. Goldcrests can come so close, it feels as if you can reach out and touch them. They prefer conifer woods where they thread their light grey nests made from lichen, hair and wool onto the underside of branches. The cuckoos leave them alone.

Just beyond the churchyard, drifting through the air was one of the most illicit scents of spring. Sweet and raunchy, somewhere between seaweed and honey, the heady drift of St George's mushrooms. I followed the scent to a cluster of half-hidden mis-shapen cream-coloured caps growing out of a verge. Morels and St George's are the only two edible earthbound mushrooms that appear in the spring and they are both delicious on toast with a few wild garlic flowers as a garnish. I have seen St George's mushrooms growing up around the base of London plane trees locked into the pavements from Holborn to Covent Garden. It is always tempting to gorge, to pick the lot, but I never take more than half. There is a field that runs down to the edge of the cliffs near Beachy Head which, in good years, is patterned with many rings of St George's mushrooms. They can live and fruit for hundreds of years, but they are becoming harder to find as more and more meadow fields are ploughed up for silage grass.

It is strange to see bare fields in late April bordered by thickening woods and hedges filling with new leaves. The fallow fields that remain are waiting for forage maize, which is drilled after the risk of the last frost is past; it is the last crop to be sown. My plan had been to follow the path that ran around the edge of Sutton Common as there was nothing on the map to indicate that a public footpath ran through the middle of it, but built into the fence was a swing gate and, beyond it, a sandy path meandering through the beginnings of bracken towards a blue horizon, holding the scuffed feathers of silver birches and the calm of Scots pines.

I love what sunshine does to commons – how it heats them up and in high summer fills them with flies, how they smell of musk and ale. They are probably at their palest in spring, when the fine-grained soil heats and cools very quickly. In the summer, they are lush with bracken, but they really flower in autumn, and even in the hardest frosts of winter the earth on the paths remains loose and doesn't freeze. From Sutton Common the view to the east spans a collection of variegated fields and, behind them, the hanger woodlands and reclining lines of the South Downs, which blurred as my eyes filled with tears. This started happening to me about four or five years ago and has happened every spring since then. It is one view that breaks me, raising tears; it is a physical shedding of the hardened layers that winter leaves. On television, it often seems that it is only the natural world which is renewed each spring: that, as human beings, we observe it but take no part in it – that spring happens in the natural world but not in us.

It is a permitted path that runs through Sutton Common. Permitted footpaths are those gifted by landowners, who have given their permission for the public to use them. On the map they are red dotted lines but the vast majority of them are not mapped, so on the ground there is happily no way of knowing where they might lead. I headed vaguely south towards the corner of the Common that slopes down past a small sandstone pit, where I skinned the fence under some pines, ending up back on the bridleway that runs around the edge of this little island of greensand.

Back on the clay, the path led through a wood still wet with last night's rain. The air was warming by the hour but it would take a month or so to dry out this path; more than long enough for the first of the mosquito larvae to lift off from the surface of the muddy coloured puddles. At some point this must have been a wider path, almost a drove, but now there are trees and brambles on either side screening the fields and cutting the sunlight into blades and shafts.

Apart from a couple of cars driving along the road next to Burton Mill and a woman walking her dog on Sutton Common, I had seen no one all morning. This part of Sussex is sometimes referred to as feeling remote, a scattering of hamlets set among yellow and brown roads. I noticed deer had left their hoof prints in the mud just before I cut over a stile and crossed a field back to Sutton. There must have been quite a few of them and they must have been travelling down this path last night through the dark, going into the depths of Hospital Copse or Swares Wood, to the feast of new leaves and fresh grass.

Spring is a season but it is also a generalisation: we have largely dictated that strawberries should share the same bed as daffodils. There is always a two-week period usually sometime around the Druidic celebration of Beltane, when spring becomes a festival of the flowering of life. It lasts for as long as the cow parsley is in bloom. but it does not begin on a certain date and end on another. What drives this rush of growth is warmth, water and light – the natural world is not subject to clocks, to minutes and weeks. The sparrows are not counting their kings; nor does the mountain measure its standing in metres. The yew is surely more an emblem of patience than of time.

Sutton, West Sussex

Start and finish: OS map 121. Grid reference 153978
Time: four hours

▶ From the church head downhill and take the path on your left. This passes a few houses and then runs over a field and down into a wood.

▶ After the wood, go over the footbridge and continue along the path until you reach a minor road: here you turn right, then about 150 yards further on take the path on your right, which leads into Barlavington.

▶ Walk through the churchyard and then turn right, following the path down past a large yew and on to a minor road. Cross the road and continue along the path through some fields until you reach a wood.

▶ Here take the path on your left: this leads down into the wood and past the waterfall before emerging onto Burton Park.

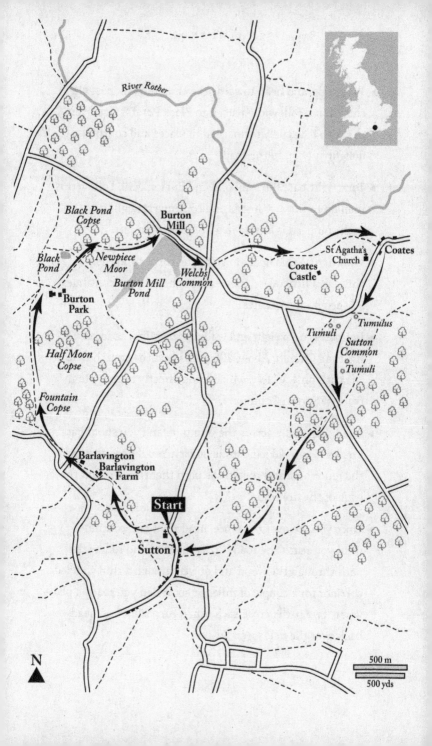

► Turn right and head towards the church. Walk past the church and follow the path into Black Pond Copse. Here the path is vaguely tarmacked in places and continues delightfully on to the road.

► Turn right past Burton Pond and Burton Mill. Follow this road up to the crossroads and continue straight over: the path you need is buried in a hedge on your left.

► Walk across this field, down to the corner and then through a little wood. Once through, the path continues all the way into Coates.

► In Coates, turn right and walk up the minor road past St Agatha's Church. About 400 yards past the church take the path on your left, which leads directly to the gate in front of Sutton Common.

► Head diagonally across the Common and you should end up next to an old sandstone quarry. You'll need to jump the fence here and re-join the path that runs around the edge of the Common.

► Once you are over the fence, head right and continue until you reach the road. Cross the road and follow the path through the wood and down through a thin wooded corridor for a couple of miles or so. When you reach a place where two paths cross each other, turn right and head back over the fields into Sutton.